A CASE FOR DUE PROCESS IN THE CHURCH

Father O'Callaghan, December 1870. This photograph was taken when he returned from the First Vatican Council.

DIVISION OF THE SOCIETY OF ST. PAUL, STATEN ISLAND, N.Y. 10314

A CASE FOR
DUE PROCESS
IN THE CHURCH

Father Eugene O'Callaghan
American Pioneer of Dissent

Nelson J. Callahan

Nihil Obstat:

    Rt. Rev. Msgr. Charles J. Ritty, J.C.L.
    Censor Deputatus

Imprimatur:

    Clarence G. Issenmann, S.T.D.
    Bishop of Cleveland
    April 30, 1970

The nihil obstat and imprimatur are official declarations that a book or pamphlet is free of doctrinal or moral error. No implication is contained therein that those who have granted the nihil obstat and imprimatur agree with the contents, opinions or statements expressed.

Library of Congress Catalog Card Number: 71-158570

SBN: 8189-0214-0

Designed, printed and bound in the U.S.A. by the Pauline Fathers and Brothers of the Society of St. Paul, 2187 Victory Blvd., Staten Island, N.Y. 10314 as part of their communications apostolate.

DEDICATION

This book is dedicated to the pioneer priests of America in whose faith, courage and hope we of a later time struggle to labor. Among them was Eugene O'Callaghan who left us a legacy of wisdom, loyalty and hope in the ancient Church of Rome

In compiling this partial record of the life and thought of Eugene O'Callaghan, I have had a great deal of support and help from many people. To all those who know of this work, I wish to express, as best I can, my deepest thanks.

But I owe special debts of gratitude to several persons whom I would like to mention by name. To the late Monsignor Michael Hynes who first suggested to me the significance of Father O'Callaghan; to the late Paul J. Hallinan, Archbishop of Atlanta who frequently urged me to write again what Eugene O'Callaghan wrote for the American Church of the late Twentieth Century and whose last words to me in February, 1968 were "Have you begun to write?"; to Father John Tracy Ellis who frequently clarified much of this material for an often confused assistant pastor; to Fathers Eugene Kane, Anthony Winters, Richard McHale, Gilbert Sheldon and Michael Murphy, Cleveland priests in the tradition of Eugene O'Callaghan who both criticized this work constructively and translated into English primary archival sources from Rome and Cleveland; to Monsignor Charles Ritty for his encouragement of this effort and for so generously accepting the difficult task of acting as my censor; to Sisters Kathryn Moran, H.M., Susan Schorsten, H.M., Mary Patrick, O.P. Dr. Eugene Best, and to Miss Patricia Lange for proofreading this manuscript and for the invaluable research they so generously supplied; to Mrs. Mary Stanton who typed this manuscript several times and who never became either bored or angry with the pace of my work; to Father Vincent A. Yzermans and Mr. Joseph

Breig who introduced me to the mechanics of publication and who suggested this format; and to Doctor Frank R. Hanrahan whose deep interest in Eugene O'Callaghan is a symbol of his deep love of the priesthood.

Finally I am grateful to my bishop, the Most Reverend Clarence G. Issenmann who encouraged me in the most candid way possible when he told me, "Let people today see our history." This I have tried to do.

But most importantly, I have been sustained by my parents, Mr. & Mrs. Nelson Callahan, by my brother Doctor Kenneth Callahan and by my sister, Mrs. Gerald Porter. They are each historians in their own right.

Contents

A CASE FOR DUE PROCESS IN THE CHURCH

Part of a group of pioneer priests of the Cleveland Diocese taken at a meeting in 1869. Father O'Callaghan is seated in the center and Father James Molony is seated at the extreme right.

Girls' first communion class at St. Colman's, Cleveland in 1896, five years before Father O'Callaghan died.

I

One hundred years ago, Father Eugene O'Callaghan —
truly a prophet of the Church in America in the last third
of the nineteenth century — was repeatedly called a rebel
priest and even a heretic because he tirelessly appealed for
changes in structures and procedures in the Church, and for a
new style in governing: changes which a century later are
gradually being made, style which finally is coming into style.

Father O'Callaghan pleaded for dialogue between bishops
and priests. He argued for collegiality: a sharing and a consulting in the exercise of authority. He urged that "due process" be established; that is, that a person accused have the
right to know the accusations, to face his accusers, to be
given a fair hearing, to be able to appeal an unfavorable decision.

Father O'Callaghan chided his own bishop and other American bishops for arbitrariness in making decisions and issuing
directives; for acting without first consulting the experience
and judgment of pastors and other priests, who were close
to the people and thoroughly informed about day-to-day problems. He noted the contrast between the often abrupt and
authoritarian methods of many bishops and the humane wisdom and courtesy of the Vatican.

Father O'Callaghan insisted on the necessity, and the
moral imperative, of giving tenure to priests in their positions,
plus assured incomes, plus care and security in sickness and
in old age. He sprang to the defense of priests who were

1

unjustly treated, including one who criticized the expenditure of the people's sacrificial contributions to impart "secular polish" to students in Catholic schools at a time when the inner-city poor (at that time whites, not blacks) were desperately in need of help.

Father O'Callaghan's bishop grew so exasperated with him that at one point he vented his feelings in his diary by writing, "I will have law and order, come what may." Yet he ended as an admirer and a fast friend of his "rebel priest."

The truth was that if Father O'Callaghan was in any sense of the word a rebel, he was the very model of the right sort of rebelliousness.

He practiced what he preached: just as he urged upon the bishops a more Christian, considerate and democratic style in governing, so did he couch his "rebelliousness" in a style that was the very perfection of dialogue.

The river of letters that flowed from his pen, and caused some to dismiss him as a "rebel" and a "heretic," sparkled with clarity and glowed with literary beauty, with reasonableness, with persuasiveness, with charity, courtesy, respect for the bishops and loyalty to them, and unbreakable love for the Church.

Never did Father O'Callaghan confuse the accidental with the essential, the changeable with the unchangeable. With penetrating intelligence and unfailing power for perceiving distinctions, he exposed the error and the danger in the thinking of persons who attacked "the institutional Church itself" rather than the things in it that needed correcting.

Father O'Callaghan, in short, was a model for the age of dialogue which has now come upon us. He criticized not persons but mistakes; he had an extraordinary ability to speak forthrightly and firmly about errors and evils without giving offense. He did not advance by destroying opponents, but by getting them to see, sooner or later, that what he was saying was true and wise.

When he saw that the errors ought to be brought into the open and openly discussed by bishops and priests and people, Eugene O'Callaghan became the anonymous author of the classic Jus Letters which were published, with tremendous impact, in *The New York Freeman's Journal.* Thus he became nationally known —or rather nationally unknown; for not until long after, in the closing years of his life, did he disclose himself, for the benefit of historians, as the writer of the famous Letters.

Then the silence and the obscurity of death came to this remarkable midwestern pastor, this extraordinary priest of the Diocese of Cleveland, Ohio, which to many at the time seemed a frontier and almost a wilderness. The great truths he had uttered seemed for a time to be all but forgotten; but the leaven he had placed in the Church was quietly and irresistibly working. The "rebel priest" was being taken in hand by time, which in due course would show that in fact he was a prophetic thinker and a sacrificial servant of God, heroically in love with the all-too-human but nevertheless essentially divine Church.

From this humble, brave, luminously intelligent and utterly dedicated man, today's Catholics can learn how to engage nobly in dialogue, and how to make fully successful such modern Church reforms as due process, collegiality, tenure and all the rest. And they can rediscover their own pioneer energies and ingenuities as they see this amazingly intellectual priest riding behind huge laboring horses, helping his people to bring into reality the parish church he inspired them to build with their own hands with stones they quarried themselves in the depths of an economic depression.

With the same hands with which he held the reins on long and exhausting journeys, Father O'Callaghan wrote such things as the following trenchant passage in one of his Jus Letters:

Editor Freeman's Journal: It was a pagan who said beautifully: The day that makes a man a slave robs him of half his virtue. And he might have added: The moment you clothe a man with unlimited power you let loose the bridle of his passions. Either extreme is depreciable. . . . While I here merely generalize, and am far from asserting that . . . a priest must be a slave, or a bishop necessarily a tyrant, I cannot deny that, through abuse, there is a tendency to either extreme implied in the relations at present existing between priest and bishop . . .

While our present system is calculated to degrade the priest, it is apt, on the other hand, to injure the bishop, by inducing a stubborn obstinacy and pertinacity in his own opinions, despite the arguments and reasons of his priests. The present system of discipline works evils in both directions, which could easily be remedied by a little measure of *law* limiting the *absolute* power of the one party, and defining a few *rights* of the other.

Let us make the acquaintance of the priest who published such amazing insights one hundred years ago.

II

In late June of 1880, Bishop Richard Gilmour decided to form a new parish out of the western part of St. Patrick's Parish on Cleveland's near west side. The pastor, Father Eugene Mary O'Callaghan, objected because he felt that the new parish was getting four streets of parishioners who were needed badly to assist in supporting a heavy debt. Bishop Gilmour responded to this protest by observing,

> there is too much of *self* everywhere, if you were in the place of the new pastor, you would expect to get these streets.

O'Callaghan had a surprising answer. He objected that if he were in the place of the new pastor, he would not expect those streets. And to prove his point, he offered to resign the pastorate of St. Patrick's and take the new parish, provided St. Patrick's kept the streets in question.

Gilmour felt O'Callaghan was merely reacting emotionally. He said he was sure this was not what O'Callaghan really wanted. O'Callaghan replied that he meant what he said; that he would begin the new parish, and he added,

> One day, Rt. Rev. Bishop, you may judge how much of *'self'* there is in my taking the blank sheet of paper that should be offered to a young man and, even in my old age, attempting to write the name of God on it.

The fiery O'Callaghan took the parish at the age of 49 at a time when the life expectancy of a priest in the United States was 37; and he made it prosper.

5

Nine years earlier, Father O'Callaghan had been suspended by the Administrator of the Cleveland Diocese, Father Edward Hannin, a suspension he considered unjust. The Administrator had sought an injunction in Civil Court to prevent a Cleveland pastor, Father James Monahan, from building a new church which Hannin considered to be too expensive. Monahan had countersued in the Court of Common Pleas.

At that time, in 1871, O'Callaghan was pastor in Youngstown, Ohio. He was considered by many to be an expert in Canon Law. The Cleveland Court subpoenaed him to give a deposition to a Notary Public in Youngstown on his view on how the dioceses in America held property. This he did.

The opinion [1] probably influenced the judge to decide in favor of Monahan. The deposition given by O'Callaghan (who was never present at the trial) became the property of the Court. It would seem that the Court broke confidence, for the deposition appeared in a Cleveland newspaper. Hannin then

---

1. That opinion said:
1) The bishop was the person in whom all church property should be entrusted. But Bishop Amadeus Rappe had resigned the Diocese of Cleveland at the close of the Vatican Council in July 1870.
2) Title to church property which the bishop holds is in trust of the congregation based on the laws of the Council of Trent and of the Fifth Plenary Council of Baltimore.
3) The bishop cannot in any way alienate the property of a congregation which he holds in trust without the consent of the congregation.
4) If a Bishop resigns (as Bishop Rappe had done) and an administrator is appointed (Father Hannin), that administrator has power in the diocese (faculties only) inasmuch as they are specified by the Congregation of the Propaganda for each case.
5) The Administration has none of the rights and powers over temporalities of a diocese as the bishop has nor does he have by virtue of his appointment full control, power, or possession over the real estate of the diocese.
6) During the vacancy of a diocese, nothing should be innovated or abrogated.

petulantly transferred Monahan, (who was at the time the senior priest of the diocese) to a country mission of less than twenty-five families. He suspended O'Callaghan *ex informata conscientia,* that is, for secret reasons.

O'Callaghan, after a month's suspension, asked Hannin to lift his censure. In his letter, dated August 2, 1871, he said:

> ... Considering the scandal which I very much fear will result from your arbitrary and unexpected act of suspending me, I ask for my congregation's sake, not for my own sake, that you reconsider your act and withdraw your censure. I ask no personal favors. It would seem that prudence would dictate that this congregation ... ought to be the last in the diocese that should be disturbed. I have done all I could to assuage the people and have both publicly and privately urged them to be patient, submissive and obedient to your order, but I fear trouble that neither you nor I may hereafter remedy. The fear of this and this alone has caused me to change my determination not to beg you to relieve me from the censure imposed by you ... I do not desire scandal and it would be no pleasure to me to see you the cause or occasion for it ... I never became a priest for any other motive than the desire of doing good. I have by God's grace, kept this in view throughout the many years of my ministry and I do not desire to presume to exercise the office of pastor one hour longer than I am assured my labors would be toward that end ... But before concluding, there is one other consideration with

---

7) Amadeus Rappe still holds the diocese in trust for the several congregations and he will continue to do so until a new bishop is appointed.

8) The administrator is not the Ordinary, but even if he were, no law existing says permission to build a new church must be obtained in writing from him.

which I must trouble you . . . Whether my censure be removed or not, I desire to know the grave sin of mine that has compelled you to inflict so great a punishment in order that I might correct and repent of it.

Hannin neither removed the censure nor did he state the charge until the day on which the hearing was held in a three-judge court of the Archbishop of Cincinnati *eight months later*.[2] At the hearing itself, O'Callaghan was given no chance to defend himself; he was told to sign a retraction of the statement he had given for the Civil Court and to make apology to the diocese for having prejudiced Monahan's parish against Hannin.

O'Callaghan did retract the court statement, but refused to admit that he had prejudiced the parish since he believed this was not true. So he remained suspended until Bishop Gilmour was consecrated Bishop of Cleveland in April 1872.

Bishop Gilmour's first episcopal act was to reinstate O'Callaghan with an offhand bit of advice to "forget the past." Ten months later, on February 11, 1873, O'Callaghan wrote Gilmour:

I have purposely deferred writing you in order that I might consider this matter long and well. My case is this:

1) I was suspended for nine months during which time my reputation, dearer to me than life itself, was at the mercy of friend and foe. Everyone was free to consider me guilty of whatever his malice or imagination suggested. During all that time I could not say for what cause I had been suspended. Father

2. Cardinal Aloysius Barnabo, Prefect of the Sacred Congregation of the Propaganda of the Faith asked Hannin to state the reasons for this form of suspension. Hannin failed to give his reason to the cardinal.

9

Hannin persistently refused even to hint at it; and my inability or apparent refusal to tell suggested something infamous. You may fairly imagine perhaps, but not really know, the burning sense of guilt of such a condition.

2) During all that time, I was deprived of salary; I albeit alone, homeless, if not friendless, was obligated to support myself or beg support from someone else. And even one time when dangerously ill, I was excluded from aid coming to me from The Infirm Priests' Fund which I had founded and of which, at the time of my suspension, I was President...

3) Even when a hearing was ordered, ... I was kept ignorant to the very day of what I was accused. What defense could a person so circumstanced make?

4) Whatever I wrote, I wrote in obedience to a subpoena from the civil court. I had no intention of doing wrong. If unwittingly, injury was done, *I was willing at any time to correct it as far as I could, regardless of fear or favor. But by the use of arbitrary power, I was deprived of due process.*

This last sentence is central to what might be called the extraordinary theme of O'Callaghan's life as a priest — his desire for justice in Church government.

On the near west side of Cleveland there stands a stark white stone Gothic church called St. Patrick's. It is 178 feet long and 150 feet high (not counting a square tower that rises above the center entrance). This church was built in 1878 and looks like most other Gothic, 1878 type churches in Cleveland and, for that matter, in most other American cities, except for one thing.

In Cleveland, stone churches of that time are made out of a dark sandstone called "Berea," since the quarry is in Berea, Ohio.

St. Patrick's is about seven miles from Berea. But St. Patrick's is made of a striking white limestone, quarried in Sandusky — which is fifty-five miles from St. Patrick's.

In 1878, the United States was in the midst of an economic depression, and the people of St. Patrick's could not afford the sandstone in Berea to build their church. The limestone in Sandusky was, for them at least, free. All they had to do was to cut the stone, haul it to Cleveland and hoist each two-by-one by-one-foot piece into place.

Their pastor, who knew the owner of the quarry in San-dusky, was bold enough to ask the people to make an incredible one hundred trips to the Sandusky quarry to haul one hundred wagon loads of stone. He persuaded them to cut the stone, to put it up, to mortar it and to worship the Lord in this house which they had built. And the people of St. Patrick's did all this.

This was the church which Eugene O'Callaghan resigned at the moment of its completion to go out to the swampland of West Cleveland to start a new parish.

O'Callaghan was then already twenty years a priest. In the new parish (which he called St. Colman) he lived in the loft of a barn which he had fitted up as a church. From the loft he could look out on a clear day and see the tower of St. Patrick's. But more; he could recall that in 1869, he had written, as an argument against the constant transferring of priests in the American Church:

supposing that all his (a pastor's) work is accomplished . . . at the very time when after years of toil and privation, he should expect a little rest and enjoyment of the fruits of his labors, he receives an episcopal edict ordering him presto to some Siberia in the Diocese where he might meditate on the folly of a priest's expectation under the present system of discipline.

Ironically, O'Callaghan was beginning to serve his seventeenth congregation in 1880.

III

It has often been said that no man ever walked an untraveled road and found it paved. The road that Father O'Callaghan walked led from Kanturk in County Cork, Ireland, to an unmarked grave in Cleveland. By a circuitous route it took him to the Black Swamp of the Maumee River in Ohio; to the University of Notre Dame in the fields of Indiana; to a horseback mission which covered forty miles in the Mahoning River Valley in Ohio; through the loneliness of suspension; to a personal reinstatement by Pope Pius IX in Rome during the stirring months of the First Vatican Council. It led him to Fremont, Ohio, to Alliance, Ohio, to St. Patrick's in Cleveland and to the new parish where he died. It led him close to the episcopacy, which he disdained.

For the most part, this was an unpaved road, and Father O'Callaghan traveled it alone. Perhaps because he was alone, he had time to think, to reflect, to write. And we have his writings because men saved them. He did not.

Throughout the fabric of O'Callaghan's life there are woven many threads of paradox. He was an advocate of law. He wrote of due process in ecclesiastical law; and yet he fell victim to the worst sort of abuse that the absence of proper ecclesiastical law in America in the nineteenth century permitted. His was the first voice clearly raised in this country in behalf of permanence and tenure for pastors — that they be allowed to remain with the congregation that they served and loved. Yet it was his lot to serve seventeen different congregations. He

13

denounced the financial insecurity of diocesan priests. He regretted that an infirm or aged priest "had right only to a pauper's grave." Yet he lived as a poor man among the poor. But when he died, his net worth was forty thousand dollars.

Interestingly enough, while the bishops he served considered him to be "positively hostile," a "rebel," and a "radical," (these words are theirs), he willed these same bishops this money to be used at their discretion. A later generation of priests, more secure, or perhaps less secure and longing for the days of beginnings, would call him a pathfinder.

In May of 1831, when Eugene O'Callaghan was born the youngest of six children, Ireland was still singing about the rising of 1798. There were still those alive who could recall Wolf Tone who had led that rising, and the gallows on which he died.

Ireland had no king and no leadership. The country had suffered from the domination of the English for more than five centuries.

Freedom in Ireland meant freedom to dream, to wish and to hope. Surely there was no real freedom; not in religion, politics, self-determination, ownership of land, opportunity, whatever. Ireland was a place to leave. In 1831, the generation which would leave was being born.

Eugene O'Callaghan lived in Kanturk, sixty miles north of Cork City, until he was sixteen. His father worked as a woolspinner in the village and tended a small plot of land outside. The land was owned by a man who lived in England and who never saw it.

Eugene O'Callaghan's mother died on this land in 1839 when her youngest son Eugene was eight years old. Records in Kanturk show that he was then enrolled in the public school. The records do not say how she died. Her gravestone says she was "Julia Foley, beloved wife of Timothy O'Callaghan, loving mother of Cornelius, Honora, Ellen, Daniel, Thomas and Eugene."

Daniel O'Connell lectured in Kanturk in 1845. He was urging resistance to the Queen. Father Theobold Matthew also lectured in Kanturk the same year. He was urging temperance. In 1845, neither temperance nor resistance to the Queen were real issues for the two thousand people living in Kanturk; the real issue was starvation.

The potato crop had failed that year; it would fail for the next nine years. There were eight million people living in Ireland in 1845. By 1853, only three million remained. Among the 2,581,000 who fled the famine to the United States was Timothy O'Callaghan, his six children and a friend of young Eugene, named James Molony.

They left in stages. Eugene O'Callaghan and James Molony went first, in 1847, probably because they were physically the best able to survive the eight weeks in steerage in a Cunard sailing ship.

Here was a real ordeal. It cost thirty-seven dollars. Days and nights were spent in the confinement and darkness of a hold intended for cargo, not people. Disease, lack of fresh air, lack of food and water (the steerage passenger was expected to bring his own food for the voyage), death possibly, but above all, uncertainty, were elements that marked their voyage.

They would all remember that voyage, the close pattern of the trip taken by most of our ancestors. Eugene O'Callaghan was six feet three inches tall and two hundred pounds, and his size may well have helped him to survive. In September, 18-47, he and James Molony arrived in America.

What was that America like?

On the national scene, great events were in motion. The clipper ships were carrying American-made goods to markets in China and were returning to Salem and Boston with delicacies from the Orient. James Polk was President. We were at war with Mexico. The country felt pride in a group of young Army officers who had distinguished themselves at places like Vera Cruz and Chapultepec. Their number included names like Robert E. Lee, Ulysses S. Grant, James Longstreet, William T. Sherman and Thomas J. (later to be called Stonewall) Jackson.

In Congress, men such as Henry Clay of Kentucky, Daniel Webster of New Hampshire and John C. Calhoun of South Carolina were becoming involved deeply and emotionally over the issue of the extension of slavery into the Western Territories. An unknown young man named Lincoln was practicing law in Illinois.

The cities of the American midwest were being opened to the swelling tide of immigrants overflowing from the cities on the Eastern seaboard. Commodore Vanderbilt was beginning to lay track for his railroad. It would go from New York to Chicago. Canals were being constructed. They were slow; but they moved things.

In September 1847, Eugene O'Callaghan and James Molony arrived in Toledo, Ohio, where they joined the gangs that were digging the Miami and Lake Erie Canal. Here they earned enough money in a year to bring the rest of the O'Callaghans out from Ireland to Toledo.

There were no Molonys left to bring out. The Molonys who were waiting for that money succumbed to starvation that winter. So close had their friendship become that Molony gave his money to the O'Callaghans.

There were two Catholic priests in the Western part of the State of Ohio in 1847. One was Amadeus Rappe; the other was Philip Foley. Rappe was a French-born missionary who had been working in the Toledo area since 1840. Philip Foley was a brother of Julia Foley O'Callaghan and Eugene's uncle. He had responded to the plea of the bishop of Cincinnati, John Baptist Purcell, for priests on the Ohio frontier. In 1843, Purcell, while visiting his home in Ireland, had invited the newly ordained Foley, then working in Mallow, seven miles from Kanturk, to come to the Ohio wilderness.

On October 10, 1847, Amadeus Rappe was consecrated first bishop of the Diocese of Cleveland. He left Philip Foley in charge of the parish in Toledo, St. Francis de Sales. There Foley began a school.

James Molony, who had done some teaching in Ireland, and Eugene O'Callaghan, who had not, were the entire faculty. Both men, not yet twenty years old, began here, it would seem, a profound concern for parochial school education. They were not always sure what to do about these schools, but they were concerned. Thirty-five years later, James Molony became the first Superintendent of Schools for the Cleveland diocese.

Philip Foley was concerned in another way about Catholic education. In 1842 Father Edward Sorin of the Fathers of the Holy Cross began a new experiment in Catholic higher education at the south shore of St. Mary's Lake in Northern Indiana. The log chapel still there today in replica tells the observer just how tenuous the University of Notre Dame was in the 1840s. In 1849 Father Philip Foley gave the University four thousand dollars as an endowment which would, he hoped, maintain two students at Notre Dame each year for twenty years. The first students he designated were Eugene O'Callaghan and James Molony.

James Molony, however, chose to remain in Toledo and teach at the school. Eugene O'Callaghan decided to go to Notre Dame. On September 9th, 1849 he enrolled at the university.

It seems that, more than any other source, Notre Dame influenced the shaping of Eugene O'Callaghan's thought. There is still preserved the list of items which he purchased there.

Things like a Hebrew Grammar (in French), a violin, strange remedies reflecting the medicine of the day, books on history and the classics, paper, ink, tickets on trains and stage coaches to go as far as Montreal to hear Thomas Darcy McGee, and to New Jersey to hear Orestes Brownson.

Eugene O'Callaghan maintained a correspondence with Brownson until Brownson's death in 1880. And at Notre Dame he met French-trained educators like Fathers Sorin, Lemonnier, Letorneau and Grangier. They introduced him to the men behind the intense intellectual ferment that gripped the Church in France — Lammenais, Lacordaire, Montalembert, Dupanloup, and above all, deMaistre.

Eugene O'Callaghan's copy of deMaistre's book, "The Pope" has every paragraph annotated, whole pages summarized and, as his later writings showed, memorized. Inside the front cover of the book there is, in Father Sorin's handwriting, this inscription: "Presented to Mr. Eugene M. O'Callaghan as first premium award, June 3, 1850 from E. Sorin."

From Judge Thomas Stanfield, a prominent Protestant layman of South Bend who was lecturing at the University, Eugene O'Callaghan learned about American law, about the separation of Church and State, and about religious pluralism in a free society.

And somewhere he heard about John Henry Newman. When he died in 1901, Eugene O'Callaghan's library, which was appraised at $4,000, contained every single book, tract, letter, or treatise which Newman had ever published. All of this seems to be important because when one reads what Eugene O'Callaghan wrote, the question arises, where did he get his ideas?

The records are not too clear, but it would seem that Eugene O'Callaghan graduated with a Bachelor of Arts degree at Notre Dame in 1853, and on June 28, 1856, he delivered a Salutatory address in Latin at a commencement at which he received a Master of Arts degree. His topic was the discipline of mind developed in the man who studies the Roman and Greek classics.

Among his fellow students were two American-born converts to Catholicism, Neil Gillespie and Walter Elliot. Both would become priests; Gillespie a member of the Holy Cross Fathers and future editor of *Ave Maria* magazine; Elliot, a Paulist Father who would write a celebrated *Life of Father Isaac Hecker*. *Both* would leave a peculiar new American mark on the historic Church of Rome.

Did they influence Eugene O'Callaghan? Father Elliot stayed with "his old friend from College days" every time he came to Cleveland. A newspaper article of the 1890's notes this: "How do friends who share the priesthood influence each other?"

And finally, while he was at Notre Dame, Eugene O'Callaghan was the president of the St. Aloysius Literary Society. In the spring of 1854, he invited Thomas Darcy McGee, Irish revolutionary member of the Canadian Parliament, to address this group. McGee did so, and on July 4, 1854, wrote this note to Mr. Eugene O'Callaghan:

accept and present to the St. Aloysius Literary Society my best thanks for the honor they have done me. I want to assure you that I value it very highly, and hope the acquaintance consummated may long continue between us.

When McGee was assassinated in Montreal in 1868, O'Callaghan the priest was an officer at the funeral Mass.

The summer of 1856 marked the turning point in the life of Eugene O'Callaghan. He returned to Toledo, where he found that Philip Foley had gone to Cincinnati continuing his loyalty to the bishop who had persuaded him to come to America, John Purcell. And in September of 1856, Eugene

O'Callaghan with James Molony entered St. Mary's Seminary, Cleveland, to study for the diocesan priesthood. Both were also assigned to teaching pre-seminary classics to immigrant young men at a short-lived college begun by Bishop Rappe called St. John's.

The Cleveland to which Eugene O'Callaghan came as a seminarian was an expanding frontier city. Tracks had been laid in the center of four streets to carry the street cars drawn by horses. None of the streets was paved however. Homes were lighted by lamps that burned kerosene or coal oil. John D. Rockefeller was a clerk in a dry goods firm. He would become, in oil mainly, one of the wealthiest men in the world. Some of the city's water came from the lake, but most of the people drew their water from pumps in their yards. Long distance travellers came to the city by train, by boat, by stage. Short distances were covered by carriage or on horseback.

There was reason to come to this city in 1855. As early as 1840 iron ore had been discovered by prospectors working for Colonel James Pickands and Mr. William G. Mather in the southern peninsula of Michigan on Lake Superior. In 1855 a lock was built at Sault St. Marie. Now iron ore could be transported to areas close to the coal fields of Pennsylvania. This coal was necessary for fuel to convert the ore to steel.

Colonel Pickands and Mr. Mather lived in Cleveland and they now began to bring the ore to furnaces in Cleveland on boats which they owned. Cleveland's entrance into the world of steel making was modest at first because unskilled labor was not available. Men were needed to unload ore from schooners that were coming down from Marquette, Michigan, to the docks in Cleveland.

Then came the Irish — thousands of them, huddling together in an Irish-town at the mouth of the Cuyahoga River. They called their shanty clusters Whiskey Island, or the Angle, or Bogstown. They were wild, boisterous, violent, and Catholic. They comprised nearly all the English-speaking element of the Catholic Church in Cleveland. They needed priests. For them and for many others not yet in sight, Eugene O'Callaghan prepared himself for the priesthood.

To appreciate the atmosphere of the Cleveland Seminary in the middle of the last century, it is as important to note the background of the professors as it is to record the authors of textbooks then in vogue. Successive rectors, both French, taught dogma; both were educated at St. Suplice in Paris. Five other professors, three from France, two from Ireland, were also Paris-educated. These European-educated men successfully trained a clergy that would spend much of its time on horseback, visiting the missions of a diocese that stretched from Indiana to Pennsylvania and from Lake Erie nearly to Columbus in central Ohio.

Twenty-three men were in the seminary with Eugene O'Callaghan. What did they learn? How did they affect one another? To the credit of the bishop, their rule contained this admonition:

> They, (the seminarians) will love and consider one another as members of one family without respect of person or distinctions of origin or nationality.

In a city which was strongly abolitionist, anti-slavery, during the terrifying years of the Buchanan administration, during the Jayhawking wars in Kansas and Nebraska, during the Harpers Ferry raid, during the hanging of John Brown, during the waning days of the Know-Nothing bigotry, during the Dred Scot decision, during the Lincoln-Douglas debates, Eugene O'Callaghan was a seminarian.

IV

On June 26, 1859, Bishop Rappe ordained five men to the priesthood. Among them were Eugene O'Callaghan and James Molony. Of himself on that day, O'Callaghan later said, "I was fully ready." He was twenty eight.

Bishop Rappe was pastor of his Cathedral. He conducted there one of four centers from which mission bands of priests attended, generally on a weekly or bi-monthly basis, the 50 missions in the area that did not have resident pastors.

Father O'Callaghan's first assignment was to the bishop's cathedral mission band and to the Seminary as a professor. For two years he ranged out from the Cathedral along a radius thirty miles from Cleveland, saying Mass in homes and frame structures — poor imitations of the New England style of architecture of the area — which Catholics called churches. During these two years, he nurtured six parishes to the point where they could support a pastor. Then he would move on.

In May, 1861, Father O'Callaghan was appointed resident pastor in Youngstown, Ohio. The Civil War had begun. The Union's need for steel had caused Youngstown to grow quickly once both iron ore and coal were discovered on the Mahoning River which bisects the city. By 1862, the Cleveland and Pittsburgh Railroad had been completed. It passed through Youngstown.

In September, 1862, Bishop Rappe was ill with fever. Father O'Callaghan, in a letter describing his progress in Youngstown, passed on this suggestion with regard to the cure of fever.

23

I have procured some prickly ash bark which I send you by parcel . . . I trust its use may completely cure you. It is to be prepared thus; put 2/3 of the quantity of the bark in 1/2 gallon of the best rye whiskey (or if you use all the bark, you must increase the whiskey in proportion). Let it remain 48 hours or longer before using it. Then begin the liquor 3 or 4 times a day in sufficiently large draughts as to feel the influences.

The bishop's life was prolonged for 15 years.

The progress report was encouraging. O'Callaghan had begun construction on a large brick church in Youngstown. He had opened a school. He had built a frame church in Niles, five miles from Youngstown along the railroad, and purchased a Protestant church in Warren some five miles further on. He was saying Mass at all three places each Sunday. He was living in a rented room above a store. He closed the letter by observing laconically,

ex-Bishop O'Connor of Pittsburgh is living with me.

By 1864, the church in Youngstown was completed and placed under the patronage of St. Columba. He had built three churches, established five missions and built one school in a period of three years.

On May 17 of that same year, O'Callaghan's old professor from Notre Dame, Father L. J. Letorneau, wrote:

Some time ago, Very Reverend Father Sorin handed me a letter from your reverence. It was a kind reply to the circular for the Alumni Organ in the Chapel. We have now artists from Chicago embellishing the Tableau with the names of donors in gold letters. I would desire very much to have your name and contribution ready before they leave. I have nearly enough to pay for the organ which costs three thousand dollars. We are all very well. Father Sorin sends his compliments. I hope we may have the pleasure of a visit from you on June 29 when the great organ will be tested . . .

O'Callaghan responded with cash on August 19. But he wrote this letter which indicated his displeasure with the method used in fund collecting. He said:

On the 17th of last May, you wrote me for my promised subscription to your 'organ fund' telling me that 'artists were embellishing a tableau with the names of donors in gold letters and desiring very much to have my name and contribution before they leave.' From this, I infer that the receipt of cash only entitled me to golden memory on your tableau.

Now, my dear sir, pardon me if I tell you that the hope of having my name inscribed on your golden tableau in no way influences me to offer a few dollars — nay the urgent desire to have my name and contribution has decidedly and solely *deferred* my writing sooner. I am not vain enough to vie for golden fame on an embellished tableau when wealth is the test of prominence. My sole motive for offering my mite was to show that I cherish a grateful remembrance of my *alma mater* and desire to see it lift itself proudly among the institutions of the Lord.

The insinuation that I hasten my contribution before the artists left has been to me assuredly, not very flattering, for I intended to perform what I promised without any such stimulus; and the *distrust* which it implies, I should rather have expected from some other quarter . . .

I desire to be remembered kindly to Father Sorin . . . I subscribe myself with the most sincere desire for the advancement of Notre Dame and the friendship of yourself.

O'Callaghan treasured his credibility dearly. The source of the worldly wealth that was his when he died seems to have been investments in Youngstown. In 1863, he began what was soon to become a very successful bank for the members of his parish. He was to write to a friend afterwards defending himself against the charge of violating church law:

> If I was guilty (of being in a business) my only sorrow is that I was not more guilty in as much as it benefited my people who could neither read nor write and for whom I could invest their money and thus help them to save and grow prosperous in a new land.

And to Cardinal Barnabo, Prefect of the Propaganda, he wrote:

> In Youngstown I found a Catholic people who were very poor; they suffered from religious indifference, addiction to alcohol . . . and no hope among the workers of iron and steel and the furnace workers. I had before my eyes the danger of an unstable people, owning nothing, who would fall away from the faith and who would leave the next generation without doctrine . . . The people began a business, a place to deposit and borrow money so that gradually, each man was able to own his own home . . . They built a school and the grace of God and the sacraments made them a stable people, industrious, and pure.

The bank was the Home Building and Loan Co. It owned, by 1869, some of the property on which was built the Youngstown Sheet and Tube Co. When the bank liquidated in 1896, it paid $3 for every penny invested by the stockholders in 1864. Father O'Callaghan was one of the original stockholders.

V

One of the realities of the priesthood on the Ohio frontier in the 1860's, difficult to understand today, was a chilling loneliness. Father O'Callaghan spoke often of the fact that, while in Youngstown, he was the only priest for fifty miles. Those priests, the men on horseback really, needed one another. To do something about this need, O'Callaghan and perhaps twelve to fourteen of his fellow priests began, as early as 1862, to get together at some rectory, generally once a month. They would leave their parishes, usually on Sunday afternoon, travel to the meeting place, sometimes more than half way across the state and stay together till Wednesday or Thursday. Large rectories were built in those days, but not to accommodate assistants; few parishes had more than one resident priest.

O'Callaghan's group met to discuss ideas for the most part. Every month three presentations were assigned to the members in the areas of Dogma, Moral and Canon Law, or Scripture. Letters concerning those meetings are still extant. So is a picture of these priests, twelve in number, on the occasion of one such meeting in the late 1860's.

The group looks formidable; O'Callaghan sits in the middle, none of the members are in Roman Collars; they all wear ties: They have Napoleonic poses; none really seems familiar with the art of posing for a photograph; some have beards; all look fierce.

If a bishop were in some way insecure, a glimpse at this picture would in no way bolster his confidence. His insecurity

27

would be reduced to real suspicion if the men in this picture
came to a Diocesan Synod in a group as they did in 1865 and
1867. If in debate, or disagreement with the bishop, they
voted in a block, or if they all represented the same point of
view which it would seem they had talked over ahead of time,
the bishop, given the fact that he was suspicious already, might
decide that there was a conspiracy among some of his clergy
against his authority. Finally, if one man spoke in the name of
such a group and publicly before all the priests, in opposition
to the policies of the bishop, that bishop might indeed regard
that priest as the chief conspirator against him.

Mention of all this is made because it would seem that by
1868, in spite of all that they both had done for the building
up of the Church in northern Ohio, this was the view that
Bishop Rappe took of one of the priests he had ordained only
ten years earlier, Father Eugene O'Callaghan.

For his part, Bishop Rappe wrote to Archbishop Martin
J. Spaulding of Baltimore a year later:

> In order to succeed in their plans, they (this group of
> Cleveland priests) formed a species of secret society of
> which the leader is Reverend E. O'Callaghan.

It would seem in retrospect that there was a very real
misunderstanding between these priests and their bishop in
Cleveland. The trouble at the synods had at its core a con-
flict in several areas. The priests contended that Bishop Rappe
was recruiting priests and seminarians from France to serve the
diocese and O'Callaghan objected that the diocese was already
twenty years old. This fact, he felt, should have indicated that
native born priests and seminarians could and should be found
to serve the special needs of the American Church.

Although foreign born himself, O'Callaghan was repelled
by the prospect of native born congregations being served by

a second generation of foreign born priests. This, he said, offended the spirit of American Protestants and would make the Catholics of America feel strange and inferior as they practiced their faith in their new country.

For O'Callaghan and his friends, there was another issue at the synods. The bishop, to enforce his decisions, was transferring pastors and thus implying a form of demotion in the mind of the people. This was a violation of due process, the priests felt, and when negotiation with the bishop became impossible, they took their case to Rome.

Father O'Callaghan said as much in a letter to James McMaster, the giant in the field of Catholic Journalism in the last century, and the editor of the *New York Freeman's Journal*. His complaint was one that focused on authority. On November 27, 1869, he told McMaster:

> The status of the Church in America is intolerable and cannot long continue. If priests had independence and prudence enough, the sentiments of bishops would soon change on this subject (the canonical status of priests in the United States in relationship to the bishops when their country was under the Congregation of the Propaganda). Without sin or scandal, they could make the regime of the bishops so burdensome that they (the bishops) would fly to the canons for relief . . . I believe I have received many more privileges from my bishop than I would have had I sneezed every time he took snuff . . . yet he would sing alleluia if I went out of the diocese. Of this I am perfectly aware and yet we are on very agreeable terms . . . Such is human nature. Weakness evokes tyranny. One poor priest before a bishop is powerless, but a cause supported by many, *if legitimate,* can hardly be ignored.

Years later, in 1887, O'Callaghan would reflect on the

stand taken by Cleveland priests and the openness of their course, when a newspaper article had called that course factious:

These men (the priests) had no selfish ends in view. They were fully satisfied with their respective places. They had nothing to gain and much to lose personally by their conscientious endeavor to advance the interests of religion. Some of them now dead, professed while living the love and confidence of their several congregations and died mourned by the laity as well as by the clergy of the diocese. Those yet living still enjoy not less the affection of their brother priests and their positions of responsibility in the Diocese, the esteem in which they are held, proves that faction, discord or scandal was and is utterly abhorrent to them. They desired the welfare of religion and exposed themselves to serious privation in urging their theme before the bishop himself. In and out of Synod, according to order and decorum, they urged their petitions . . . .

However much Father O'Callaghan was involved in his Youngstown parish and its missions, or in diocesan affairs in 1868, he began that year a work which would touch the core of the bishop-priest problem of authority of his day and indeed, which would change his own life also. He began to publish a series of articles which appeared as letters to the editor of the *New York Freeman's Journal.*

The general title of the series was "The Status of the Clergy." There were twelve articles in all; they were printed on the front page of the *Freeman's Journal;* they generally ran two columns. O'Callaghan chose to remain their anonymous author and signed all the articles simply "Jus."

The "Jus Letters," as they were called, attracted immediate, and widespread attention. They said with vigor and eloquence what many American priests felt regarding the relationship existing between priests and bishops, and about episcopal exercise of authority. They exposed, too, the lack of legislation that should have existed for the aged or infirm priests. O'Callaghan insisted that there, each bishop was bound in justice, not charity.

Tenure for pastors was another topic. Suspension without due process under law was another. Subsidiarity was discussed. O'Callaghan argued that a bishop really had only his priests to govern, and that if he did this well, the laity would aid the priest with joy and enthusiasm.

It was as Jus that Eugene O'Callaghan made a great contribution to the American Church in 1868-1870. The astonishing thing is that what he wrote then seems just as relevant and perhaps even more urgent today.

O'Callaghan described the background for these letters nearly thirty years afterwards when, in a letter written to the editor of the *Freeman's Journal* on August 24, 1896 he acknowledged that he was Jus. He said:

> . . . the occasion that called forth those letters was the following. At the time some improvements were introduced into the legislation of the Church in Canada, I wrote a letter to the *Freeman*, signed JUS inquiring why the Church in the United States should not have similar advantages.

James McMaster of the *Freeman's Journal* had begun a quiet campaign one month before the first Jus letter, in October 1868, in behalf of what he called parochial rights. He began by saying only a layman could defend these rights; priests were too much in jeopardy if they did so. This may explain why O'Callaghan chose to remain anonymous as Jus. In any case

Jus proved the most able champion of those rights in that day, and McMaster never really had to pursue the topic further; Jus did it for him.

The articulation of these themes marked the distillation of the reaction of the clergy to the decree of the Second Plenary Council of Baltimore in 1866 in which the American bishops had asked Rome "for twenty years more, *or perhaps forever* missionary status for the United States."

One consequence of such status was to give the bishops all but absolute authority in law over the clergy, suspending the existing canon law and abrogating all forms of recourse by the clergy except direct appeal to Rome.

Both Jus and McMaster advocated that a representative of the American clergy go to Rome during the First Vatican Council armed with a petition signed by several thousand priests from the United States. In McMaster's words the plan was this:

> That one or two priests, with the consent of their ordinaries go to Rome and at an early stage of the approaching Council, see that the respectful wishes and convictions of a large part of the clergy of this country be presented to the Holy Father.

O'Callaghan urged:

> Let the priests of America seriously consider this: Any manifestation of their desire, couched in humble and respectful language, breathing a spirit of charity, professing unalterable attachment to the Holy See, and humbly petitioning for law and protection would, I have no doubt receive a favorable hearing in Rome and move the heart of the saintly Pius IX.

The response of a large number of American priests to

these appeals seems to have been positive but uncoordinated. Some sent money, some actually did assemble petitions. Nearly all urged McMaster to persuade the anonymous Jus to assume the task of carrying the issue personally to Rome.

But unfortunately, Jus, Father O'Callaghan, ran into a problem in his own diocese. In October 1869, Bishop Rappe, angered that O'Callaghan had failed to pay one-fifth of his seminary tax, transferred O'Callaghan to Lima, Ohio. The priest protested that this sudden and unexpected act of the bishop was, in fact, a demotion, and he refused to go until he appealed to the Archbishop of Cincinnati who had already left for the Council. Then O'Callaghan asked Bishop Rappe if he might go to Rome to make his appeal.[3]

---

3. The archives of the Propaganda, now available indicates clearly that O'Callaghan presented a rather lengthy but a simple appeal to Rome, that he be reinstated as pastor of Youngstown. In the appeal he complains against his bishop's arbitrary use of power, maladministration in the seminary and vindictiveness on the part of the bishop. *C. F. Propaganda Archives Congressio Centrale*, Vol. 23, pp. 333ff.

There is no evidence that substantiates the statement of an earlier historian of the Diocese of Cleveland that O'Callaghan ever made any other charge in Rome against Bishop Rappe. *C. F.* G. F. Houck, *History of the Diocese of Cleveland*, 1903, p. 191ff.

VI

With permission of his bishop, O'Callaghan left for Rome on November 7, 1869. He had spent two days in New York with McMaster at the Church of the Transfiguration where the pastor, Father James Trainor was a staunch advocate of the themes of the Jus Letters. Only Trainor, McMaster and Molony in Cleveland knew that O'Callaghan was Jus.

Thus it was that by the beginning of January, 1870, Father O'Callaghan was in Rome, and he stayed there all during the stirring months when the First Vatican Council was in session.

Seven hundred bishops from all over the Catholic world had assembled for the first General Council of the Church in 300 years. Over 60 were from the United States. O'Callaghan was there as Jus, hopefully to forward the cause he had advocated for two years in the *Freeman's Journal*. He was also there, in his words:

> to appeal from an act of my bishop in removing me without cause on my part.

In this latter cause, he was successful. On October 13, 1870, after the Council had been prorogued, he wrote to the councilmen of St. Columba's Parish in Youngstown:

> I will sail for New York before the first of November and will resume my duties as Pastor in Youngstown . . . I am most anxious to be home again and to resume my labors and complete what has been interrupted by my departure. I have no reason to regret my visit to Rome; on the contrary, it was the Holy Father who told me to return to labor for you.

35

This was written from Kanturk in Ireland. It was the second and the last time he went back to Ireland. He was appalled by the emptiness and desolation he saw there. In that same letter he wrote:

> You would not recognize the place of our birth. The land is empty; the West and the South are deserted. Ireland is no longer alive. Our only hope is in America.

His efforts in Rome for the cause of Jus are more difficult to ascertain. In his own words, from the letter to the *Freeman's Journal* of August 24th, 1896, revealing himself as Jus, O'Callaghan described his course in Rome thus:

> I suppose it is well known that Jus went to Rome in 1869 to forward the cause he advocated in the *Freeman's Journal*. While at Rome, it was my good fortune to become acquainted with a certain Italian bishop, a member of one of the great orders of the Church, the bosom friend of Pius IX and who was afterward raised to the Cardinalate. This good bishop had access at all times to the Holy Father and used to spend many evenings with him at the Vatican. Circumstances enabled me to render him important service and thus I became quite intimate with him, visiting him whenever I chose. Need I say that I again and again spoke of the abnormal condition of the Church in America? And is it too much to believe that these pleadings reached the ear of the Holy Father?
>
> I was also fortunate in having as an old friend, an official of another great order of the Church, who held high office in one of the most important Congregations of the Church. Good fortune could scarcely procure me more influential patrons.

One wonders who his two Roman friends were.

Father O'Callaghan did return to Youngstown and was working there when Father Hannin suspended him in the summer of 1871. He was reinstated by Bishop Gilmour in April 1872 and was assigned to St. Joseph in Alliance, Ohio as pastor *pro tem.* In July 1872, he was appointed pastor of St. Ann's in Fremont, Ohio. Here he seems to have made a new start.

Fremont was a small town in the western part of the state, but an old town as towns were measured in the last century. It had been a headquarters for Rogers' Rangers in the 1760's when they made a punitive raid on the Indian Settlement near Sandusky at a time when the only white men in northern Ohio were voyageurs, trappers, and British soldiers. Fremont was not an industrial town as was Youngstown, and, although the railroad passed through the place, there was generally little reason for the trains to stop there. But in 1872, Fremont was the home of Rutherford B. Hayes.

In 1876 Hayes was elected to the Presidency of the United States, and as President he attended Father O'Callaghan's farewell party when he left Fremont in 1877 to go to St. Patrick's in Cleveland. This fact is the only one that gives any clue as to Father O'Callaghan's personal knowledge of men prominent in American civic or political life. But it would seem the presence of Hayes must have been based on friendship. Few priests have an incumbent President attend a personal social event.

At St. Ann's in Fremont, Father O'Callaghan continued to manifest, in the face of a national depression, his interest in parochial education. He built a school that still stands there.

It was also while at Fremont that Father O'Callaghan relinquished interest he had begun earlier in two other activities in the diocese.

In 1869, a group of laymen in the Youngstown area began publishing a newspaper they called *The Celtic Index*. It was financed by six priests; the largest block of stock was held by Father O'Callaghan. He contributed several articles to its columns, two of some import, on the meaning of the Vatican Council, written while he was in Rome. In the first article, he alluded to the inopportunist stance on papal infallibility taken by Archbishops Peter Kenrick of St. Louis and John B. Purcell of Cincinnati. He went on to say:

> The great and absorbing topic of conversation at present is the question of the infallibility of the Pope. There are no longer neutrals; all are divided either pro or con. The congregations of the Council are becoming less frequent than formerly. The bishops are supposed to prepare their subjects at their lodgings and come fully prepared by prayer and study, to act on the subjects of the schematica. It is said that after Easter, and before the critical voting, a great many missionary bishops will be permitted to return home . . . . The papers announced that yesterday there would be a grand requiem Mass for the repose of the soul of Montalembert who died here in Rome last week. It was also asserted that Bishop Dupanloup would preach the panegyric. All the French in Rome and many non-French appeared to flock to the church at the appointed time. I was among them. But a simple scrap of paper pinned to the door of the church said the funeral service . . . would not be held. The reason for the change is the subject of great speculation. Some say it was countermanded by special order of the Pope.

This was written on March 16, 1870, by a visitor in Rome who seemed well aware of what was going on in the City.

On March 26, 1870, he wrote to *The Celtic Index*:

> . . . The question of the infallibility of the Pope is convulsing the assembled Prelates although not introduced yet

formally. It has strong opposition and will give rise to a great deal of bad will. But it will be introduced.

The question *de ecclesia* is now up for deliberation and afterwards comes *de Summo Pontifici.* There are many grave reasons offered *contra* and many objections. But I understand that each party gives the opposition party credit for consideration and sincere motives. Notwithstanding this, there is a great deal of excitement and it would seem, from a long conversation I had with one bishop, these are not unreasonable objections *especially as to the manner in which some of the committees were formed.* (Italics his)

(It was precisely on this last point that Cardinal Lienart of Lille made his historic intervention during the first day of the first session of the Second Vatican Council.) O'Callaghan's letter went on:

I trust and pray that the result may be peaceful and the end productive of harmony.

I attended a lecture given by Bishop Dupanloup at which he said that at least half of the French and German bishops, men of ability, are opposed at least, to the opportuneness of any declaration of personal Papal infallibility, or infallibility *ex cathedra* other than the intermediate belief already existing.

... If I can send you more information without breach of faith, honor or confidence, be assured I will do so. To do more, even if I were able, would, I know, be offensive to you.

In any case, by the spring of 1874, Bishop Gilmour had determined to found a diocesan newspaper. Father O'Callaghan persuaded the stockholders and publishers of *The Celtic Index* to sell their subscription and advertising lists to the bishop and to aid him in launching, on July 4, 1874, the *Catholic Universe*. That paper is still published today.

The second involvement relinquished by Father O'Callaghan while he was in Fremont, was the office of president of the Priests' Infirm Fund.

In 1865, after the Clergy Retreat, Bishop Rappe met with a group of priests, headed by Father O'Callaghan. He listened to their concern about the problem of support for aged, infirm and retired priests, and gave his approval to their proposal. Theirs was a good plan; every priest who wanted to participate in the program was assessed 5 per cent of his yearly income. The parishes of the diocese were assessed $1 per family per year for every priest in residence at the parish. The clergy elected a board of directors to administer the fund created, to invest it, and to decide who would be eligible for benefits. The bishop was invited to participate; he was not eligible to hold office.

During a period of nearly fifty years when bishops had no responsibility in law to support their sick or aged priests, the Priests' Infirm Fund did the job in Cleveland. When Father O'Callaghan resigned as its president in 1873, he had held office for four successive terms.

There is considerable correspondence between Father O'Callaghan and Bishop Gilmour covering the period O'Callaghan was in Fremont. Most of it is routine: requests to borrow, payment of taxes (one notices that the Peter's Pence was very substantial for the size of the parish), a note thanking Gilmour for lifting the suspension under which he found O'Callaghan in 1872.

There is one curious letter. O'Callaghan speaks of a conversation he had with the bishop in which he and Father Molony were considering a suggested year's leave of absence to go to Europe to recruit seminarians for the Cleveland diocese.

O'Callaghan and Molony did not go on this mission, primarily it would seem, because they continued to maintain that the diocese was mature enough to produce its own clergy. The incident points up however, the fact that these two priests (and this is true of many others in all dioceses), immigrants, and comparatively young by today's measure, took it upon themselves to look to the next generation of priests in America. The idea of having a native-trained, native born clergy recurs constantly in the chronicle of the efforts of American priests and bishops in the last century.

On May 1, 1877, Bishop Gilmour appointed Eugene O'Callaghan to the pastorate of St. Patrick's parish in Cleveland. This was the largest parish in the diocese and the most heavily burdened by debt. The foundation of the church had been laid; the cornerstone was set in place in 1871. But the depression that chilled the country in the 1870's had frozen the church in its growth at ground level.

O'Callaghan's achievement at St. Patrick's was primarily one of administration and of building. Here, when he was in his late 40's, he joined with his people in the work of raising their church. He often drove the wagons on the trip to Sandusky for the stone. He consolidated the parish debt and reduced it by $30,000 with money collected from men who imposed upon themselves meatless Wednesday and breadless Friday for the church building fund. These men earned $14 a week, working on the ore docks by the river below the bluff upon which the church still stands.

At St. Patrick's, Father O'Callaghan had his first assistant, and instead of renting a room for quarters, he built a small house where the two men lived. This was a long way indeed from the loneliness of the outrider missions in Youngstown.

The O'Callaghan correspondence, while he was at St. Patrick's, is full of items which were new to him, but routine by today's standards. Some of these letters, quite candid, are to the bishop, but the issues they explore are quite local in meaning and are somewhat irrelevant today. They do reflect, however, a bit of the reluctance of the early missionary priests of America to submit to a growing central Diocesan Curia.

While he was at St. Patrick's Father O'Callaghan began to receive appointments to some minor offices, as Bishop Gilmour started to organize a Curia. When the need for uniformity in the schools gradually emerged as a pressing demand, the bishop made him an examiner both of teachers and of students. And when Rome urged American bishops to organize examinations for the junior clergy, O'Callaghan was appointed to this board also.

By 1880, the aged Archbishop of Cincinnati, John Purcell, was fully ready to receive a coadjutor. A *terna* was presented to Rome with the names of candidates for that position. In June of that year Ella Eddes, a correspondent in Rome for several bishops in America, wrote James McMaster at the *Freeman's Journal* that the three names sent to Rome were those of Bishop William Elder of Natchez, Bishop James Fitz-gerald of Little Rock and O'Callaghan.

There is no evidence that O'Callaghan was ever considered seriously by Rome. But on the subject of his possibility of being a bishop, O'Callaghan wrote McMaster in this very same year:

> I envy not the lot of those who are burdened with this terrible responsibility. If I can do my duty as a simple priest and try to aid the few souls committed to my care, I find I have plenty to do without exposing my own salvation and that of multitudes of others, as would be the case were I a bishop ... A mitre, would cause my head to be heavy indeed, but my heart heavier yet .... I am happy when men of greater ability are chosen ... For me, I have this am-

bition, to live long enough to see the relations between the First and Second order of the hierarchy regulated by law.

One wonders why O'Callaghan showed such reluctance to assume responsibility on the level where his qualities of leadership and insight, as well as his scholarship, might have been productive of great good for the Church in America.

It was in June of 1880, that O'Callaghan resigned the pastorate of St. Patrick's just at the moment when the parish was on the verge of its prosperous years. As was said in the first paragraph of chapter two the issue regarding the boundary lines was one of principle for him. It seems he had no regrets in going out to found one more parish, St. Colman's. Here he spent the last twenty-one years of his rather eventful life, in comparative calm. Between 1880 and 1887, his parish had less than 100 families. When he died in 1901, however, St. Colman's was becoming what it would be by 1920, the largest parish in the Cleveland diocese.

There was administration and building involved in the work of the priest at St. Colman's but these aspects of O'Callaghan's work there were not burdensome. His role in his final years was primarily pastoral. This seemed to be what he wanted most as he told Bishop Gilmour:

> . . . I prefer a small place. It is good enough for me and affords a field, really, for more zeal than I possess.

At St. Colman's O'Callaghan built a church, a school and a rectory. All were frame buildings; they are gone today. The people who first settled there were very poor; they represented the second wave of Irish immigration that broke over the American midwest. These people were from the western counties of Ireland. The parish bulletin calls attention every January to the fact that "the pastor will begin a weekly course that will last nine months on how to read and write the English language."

During these years, O'Callaghan celebrated the 25th and 40th anniversaries of his ordination. On both occasions, he and James Molony left town for the day, as he said:

> to escape even the slightest demonstrations. These we do not need; nor do the people.

But every month, usually on the first Sunday, he would have a buffet dinner at his house, to which all priests who wished to come, were invited. The invitation read:

> We will discuss ideas. We will not talk about people. We will try to inform one another and share our views . . . Please come . . . May there be no lonely rectories on Sunday evenings.

The ideas that continued to dominate the life of Father O'Callaghan may have had substantial ventilation at these gatherings. In any case, these ideas were developed at length in his correspondence during his years at St. Colman's.

On Sunday night, March 10, 1901, Father O'Callaghan did not host a buffet dinner. That night he died. Six months earlier he told Bishop Ignatius Horstmann, the last Cleveland bishop he would serve:

> I lately underwent a very severe surgical operation for the extraction of a tumor on my right side. It was not successful. I cannot use my right hand. I apologize for not returning my census report in due time.

He was right-handed. He wrote that last letter with his left hand.

In his will he stated:

> I commend my soul to God who made me; and my body

to the earth to be buried with as little expense as possible, encased in a plain wooden coffin with no marker at my grave.

These instructions were carried out. The will continued:

... The residue of my estate, real and personal, I bequeath to the Roman Catholic Bishop of Cleveland for the purpose of establishing a home for homeless boys to be under Roman Catholic government.

The estate was $40,000. The bishop built the home for homeless boys. It still stands. Among its administrators were the late Bishop Hubert LeBlond of St. Joseph, Mo., and the present bishop of Lafayette, Indiana, Bishop Raymond Gallagher.

At the funeral of Father O'Callaghan Bishop Horstmann said:

He shared the labors of the faithful priests who guarded the household of the faith. A pioneer and a pathfinder, he carried the Lord to Catholics isolated often in the poverty of the immigrant. The times needed men of strength with stout hearts and piercing hope to bear the awful burdens of life on the American frontier.

After the funeral, Father James Molony planted a tree on the grave of his friend of more than 60 years. That tree is forty feet high today and Molony is buried next to it.

VII

At the close of his life, forty years after he had been ordained a priest, Father Eugene O'Callaghan reflected, very briefly, on the role that honest dialogue must play in the relationship that should exist between bishops and priests. In 1896, he said:

> I believe today it may be probable that our venerable bishops only desire to be made acquainted with the *true* wants of the inferior clergy, in order to begin their amelioration. . . let us always be expectant, and convey our expectancy to those whose duty it is to serve.

He could say this as he looked back on his own life which was marked often with some real collisions with the bishops he served in the diocese of Cleveland. But these collisions occurred only when issues were at stake which involved principle. It is as interesting to note the things Father O'Callaghan chose to ignore as it is to note the issues upon which he took a stand. While he seemed to ignore past struggles, whether won or lost, his focus had an insistent nowness. He seemed to begin with this premise which he wrote in 1869:

> Priests have intelligence. Knowledge with them is quality *sine qua non* . . . They need it in the exercise of their profession; they spend, even as does the bishop, their whole lifetime in its pursuit. Were they not possessed of it, the bishops would sin seriously in permitting them to minister to a congregation. Were a priest to lack knowledge,

47

the bishop should immediately withdraw the faculties of that priest. So priests know the law as well as the bishop does; they know his duties as well as he knows theirs ... They know where legitimate authority ought to stop and where usurpation may begin. They know the weaknesses and prejudices of human nature, and are able generally to assign acts to their true motives, no matter what ostensible reasons may be given to justify them. And it is hard for intelligent subjects, thus instructed, to submit to acts justified by no law, and perpetrated simply in the absence of all law and proceeding solely from the mind of one not much more distinguished for knowledge than themselves. The ignorant or the simple may not always distinguish between law and arbitrary will, but it is otherwise with the intelligent. With priests who are the peers of the bishops in knowledge, every act unwarranted by law ... *is noticed.*

The fact that the acts of the bishop were noticed by the priests caused Bishop Richard Gilmour of Cleveland to complain to O'Callaghan in September 1884:

I admit you may find some things in my administration you may deem severe, but see things as I have and you will calmly and honestly say with me, I have done nothing from a motive of revenge or to wound.

O'Callaghan replied:

You have not allowed me or any of your priests to 'see things as I have.' I do not refer to matters which require secrecy; that of course is your burden. I refer to matters which concern the Church in this diocese. Your process of policy and of decision (making) occurs in your mind alone. Yet we all must share the results of this policy and decision (making). Is this fair to you? Is it fair to your priests who labor with you? If we share the results, we will have to share the process by which they were achieved. You must let us know what you are doing and why. The good of the Church demands this.

A year later, in 1885, O'Callaghan suggested to the bishop:

Call your priests together once a year; review the past year's work; outline the work for the coming year. Ask us for suggestions . . . Perhaps we cannot help, but we would be happy to share at least your concern. A later generation of both clergy and laity may demand this from one of your successors.

The bishop did not follow this suggestion. Both he and O'Callaghan were immigrants; Gilmour from Scotland; O'Callaghan from Ireland. Both were educated from their adolescence in America. But the priest grasped the American bent toward consensus better than the bishop. The puzzling question is why the one and not the other? But at least the priest was in honest dialogue with the bishop who was listening, if not acting.

There was a tone of fierce loyalty in the opposition O'Callaghan leveled at his bishops. There was also respect in this opposition, and he took careful pains to avoid being misunderstood by the bishop. O'Callaghan took such pains in a letter of January 2, 1874 to Bishop Gilmour in which he wrote:

I have intended to write you on a matter of personal explanation and now avail myself of this opportunity to do so. When I last saw you, in company with Fathers Sidley and Molony when you were so good as to give us a year's leave of absence so that we might seek seminarians for the diocese of Cleveland in Europe, you said we could do so provided we could find priests to take our place . . . I thanked you, saying, 'I thank you bishop for your permission, as far as it goes.' Fathers Sidley and Molony thought this expression was offensive and called it to my mind. I assure you, Right Reverend Bishop, I had not the remotest idea of giving offense or of expressing anything else than gratitude . . . My expression if fully said, would be this: 'although you cannot positively assure us now that we may go, yet as far as you permit us, dependent upon contingent circumstances within your control, I thank you.'

My expression may have sounded harshly to you . . . I meant to express my unfeigned thanks.

Unfortunately, I know that many of my expressions may be suspicious to some persons, and on this account I ought to be more circumspect. But whenever I know or even suspect I have been misunderstood, I feel it my duty (and especially to my superiors) to explain myself.

It was this same sense of loyalty and candor that permeated a letter O'Callaghan wrote Gilmour in protest in January, 1879. That year the bishop had given territorial lines to a French nationality parish in Cleveland which bordered St. Patrick's territorial parish of which O'Callaghan was pastor. The reason for the protest was that the bishop gave the French parish streets which belonged to St. Patrick's.

O'Callaghan obeyed the bishop's order and announced the new boundary to the people. Then he protested in a letter to the bishop which listed thirty-two reasons why these English-speaking people should not be attached to a French-speaking church. He closed that letter by saying:

In conclusion, My Lord, while believing in the purity of your intentions and asserting before God the sincerity of my own, I again, humbly but earnestly repeat my protest . . . .

What he did not say was that there were no French-speaking Catholics living on these streets.

The bishop rescinded his order.

A far more serious exchange developed between O'Callaghan and Bishop Gilmour in late 1879 regarding a diocesan community of religious women. Gilmour's predecessor, Bishop Amadeus Rappe, in 1851, had founded the Sisters of Charity of St. Augustine. Its members opened a home for orphans in Cleveland that same year. In 1864, Bishop Rappe appealed for public funds, which he got, to open St. Vincent Charity Hospital. The Sisters staffed the hospital.

In 1870, Bishop Rappe resigned the diocese of Cleveland. But before he left Cleveland, he gave the deed of title to the hospital to the Sisters, who then formed a legal corporation made up of nine of their members called "The St. Vincent Charity Hospital Corporation."

In 1878, Bishop Gilmour asked the Sisters for the deed to the hospital. He had a good reason for asking. He wanted to establish a number of neighborhood clinics which would give out-patient care to the poor. Those requiring bed care would be taken by diocesan ambulances to the hospital. The diocese would own the clinics and the hospital; it would assume the burden of fee collecting and the Sisters would be free to do bed care. And there would be no proliferation of Catholic hospitals in a rapidly expanding city.

The Sisters, however, refused to sign over the deed. They also refused to tell the bishop who the nine members of the hospital corporation were. The bishop tried persuasion and failed. Then he removed the Blessed Sacrament from their convent chapel and forbade Mass to be said there.

At this point, the Sisters asked Father O'Callaghan for counsel. Their convent was within the confines of his parish and they did the sacristy work in St. Patrick's church.

O'Callaghan told the Sisters to advise the bishop that they would appeal to Rome. They did so, and Gilmour, feeling, it would seem, either that he was justified or that the Sisters would not know how to present a petition in Latin to the Propaganda, told them to go ahead.

O'Callaghan wrote the petition, translated it into Latin, and sent it to Rome. Within two months, a ruling came back from the Propaganda. It said the Sisters' chapel was to be re-opened for divine services and that the matter of the title to the hospital was to be adjudicated by the Archbishop of Cincinnati.

Gilmour was upset. On December 23, 1879, he wrote O'Callaghan:

> ... by counsel and assistance and by making your rectory a meeting place for priests and Sisters, you have done all you could to destroy episcopal authority over a religious community with which you had nothing to do . . . Considering the unjustifiable attack you have made upon me through the Sisters and the encouragement you gave them and also your refusal to pay your share of the priests' retreat of 1878, I cannot help but think that my belief that you are trying to destroy authority . . . is supported by ample proof . . .

> It is a sad state of affairs when a bishop is forced to feel a few of the priests of his diocese are waiting and watching to trip him up, and that if there is a shadow of a case on which they can hang a charge, they are ready to enter the field against him. This you did in the case of the Sisters and in your refusal to pay your just share of the expenses of the last retreat . . . Of course you will consider this letter severe . . . but it is time to call halt . . . when you are so ready and active to help others in their . . . efforts to resist lawful authority . . . .

O'Callaghan replied on January 9, 1880:

My duties during the Christmas season prevented me from answering your favor of the 23rd of December sooner. It is true that I did not pay the fifteen dollars for the four and one-half days of entertainment during the *retreat* in the summer of 1878 because I considered it exorbitant. I do not consider this disobedience to episcopal authority for many reasons that will suggest themselves to your Lordship. To all the other charges in your letter inasmuch as they concern me, I not only plead 'not guilty,' but I deny them specifically. It is much easier to prefer accusations than to prove them.

I thank you for all your kindness has led you to do for me. I thank you also for your letter which I sincerely believe contains your frank and candid opinion of me.

If all you state in your letter is true, then God aid and comfort you, you are a badly persecuted bishop; if not true, then God aid and comfort those you consider your enemies. They are a badly maligned body of priests. In any case, I wish you most sincerely a Happy New Year.

Bishop Gilmour did not reply. One wonders why O'Callaghan did not choose to pursue the reasons for his involvement in the Sisters' case. Was it because, as the bishop said, it was really not his business? Or was it because O'Callaghan had succeeded in negating an act of arbitrary and cruel use of power by the bishop and had placed the case in a juridical context? If this were so, then the freedom of law, not beating the bishop, was O'Callaghan's goal.

O'Callaghan and Gilmour encountered one another again in 1880. For O'Callaghan the issue was the same as it had been with the Charity Sisters, the misuse of arbitrary power, but in this case, this power was used against a priest who was a close friend of O'Callaghan's.

Father John Quinn was from the same town in Ireland as O'Callaghan, Kanturk in County Cork. He had been educated for the priesthood at St. Patrick's Seminary at Maynooth and at St. Mary's Seminary in Clèveland. He was ordained in 1854.

After a brief tour of missionary work in the Toledo area, he was appointed a professor of Theology at St. Mary's Seminary in Cleveland. In 1864 he was made its rector. In 1866 he was assigned as pastor of a parish in Toledo, Immaculate Conception. Here he built a church and school and all seemed to be going well when the financial depression of 1877 struck with full force the struggling wage earners of Toledo.

In 1878 a dialogue began by letter between Quinn and Bishop Gilmour which tells the story best.

Gilmour to Quinn on January 5, 1878:

You are hereby appointed as one of the examiners of the junior Clergy. The tests will be held at the Seminary in Cleveland on February 2nd and 3rd beginning each day at 9 A.M.

Quinn to Gilmour January 11, 1878:

I wish you would excuse me from attending the examinations at the Seminary on February 2nd and 3rd. The fact is that it is impossible for me to make any preparation. My time is entirely occupied with the burdens of the congregation... I fear that our receipts for 1877 will fall below the actual expenses including interest on the current debt... I may be forced to close the higher school for want of money to pay the teacher...

Gilmour to Quinn March 14, 1878:

I forbid you to close your higher school... Such a suggestion is scandalous and is contrary to all law.

Quinn to Gilmour April 4, 1878:

Last Friday I dismissed the higher boys school simply because I am unable to pay the teacher any longer... I could continue I suppose by borrowing more money but this would rectify itself when my credit and ability to pay would be exhausted... I do not intend to contract obligations which I cannot meet except by extorting money from those who now are scarcely able to provide means for their subsistence. If my resolve to contract no debts which I cannot see my way clearly to pay is the occasion of scandal, I must plead guilty without the extenuating circumstance of sorrow for the offense. If such a course be scandal, there are many congregations in this country to whom it would have been a blessing had they been so scandalized for it would have saved them from the bankruptcy which now stares them starkly in the face...

The debts of the church I consider a strict obligation of justice; the support of the schools, a work of charity to be assisted from the surplus revenue of the church where parents are unable to pay. I see no reason why so much, not only of the surplus, but even of the necessary revenue of the church should be expanded in giving not just religious instruction, but even a very high secular polish to the rising generation to the almost total exclusion of the feeble suffering and deserving poor of our central cities. These people are almost as much ignored by our church as if they did not exist at all.

Here was an appeal for dialogue from a former seminary rector. But Gilmour failed to see the signal and treated the case as one to be solved by the use of power. After confrontation, Gilmour missed an opportunity to negotiate, in this instance, on tuition for parochial school attendance.

Gilmour to Quinn April 8, 1878:

I hereby order you to reopen your higher boys school immediately. You have by your false teaching violated all law and flaunted authority in your recent act of defiant rebellion.

Quinn to Gilmour April 9, 1878:

If I open the school, I wish to know if it shall be a free school or a pay school? If as a free school, since the present revenue of the church is not adequate to pay the expenses, how shall the teacher be paid? . . . I have had no salary for two years; shall I secure church debts? . . . I need no permission from my bishop to discharge an employee who up to now has been paid by me . . . I consider your letter to be the grossest insult I have received since I became a priest . . . You do not merely say I was wrong or too cautious or even negligent. You say I hold and teach false doctrine and that I am a defiant rebel. Now I demand as an act of simple justice that you prove these accusations against me or retract them. You have my letter; send it with this to the Most Reverend Archbishop of the Province or to whomever you may appoint to examine this matter. If I have taught false doctrine or denied any Catholic truth I will make ample retraction; if I have been falsely accused, I will expect reparation . . . .

Gilmour to Quinn, April 30, 1878:

I hereby transfer you from the pastorate of Immaculate

conception, Toledo to the pastorate of St. Mary's Church, Wakeman, Ohio. . . .

Wakeman was a parish of thirty families. It had no school.

Quinn to Gilmour, May 2, 1878:

I will, *Deo volente,* be in Wakeman on the 19th of May. I have appealed to the Archbishop of Cincinnati.

Quinn to Gilmour, March 5, 1880:

I respectively wish to inform you that I have made recourse to Rome and, unless he is unacceptable to you, Reverend Eugene O'Callaghan of St. Patrick's, Cleveland will act as my counsel . . . .

As O'Callaghan had written in 1869:

. . . with priests, who are the peers of the bishop in knowledge, every act unwarranted by law *is noticed.*

Now twice within a year, he was involved as a counsellor to those who felt themselves wronged by the misuse of arbitrary episcopal power. And twice, O'Callaghan's counsel was to go to Rome for recourse.

This time also, Rome ordered the case to be adjudicated by the Archbishop of Cincinnati. In the case of the Sisters of Charity, the adjudication took place. In the case of Father Quinn, represented by O'Callaghan, Bishop Gilmour simply kept stalling. O'Callaghan wrote in 1884 to Gilmour in behalf of Quinn:

The Archbishop of the Province has appointed a commission of investigation and my client, Reverend J. Quinn, respectfully asks that the hearing ordered by Rome be begun . . . He is not well and wishes that a statement of charges be submitted by you in order that we might prepare a defense . . . He has now been kept waiting for almost *five years* for you to make this presentation . . . Rt. Reverend Bishop, I ask you, is this honest?

Quinn indeed was not well. In May 1884 he suffered a paralytic stroke. He was taken to a hospital in Toledo where he died in 1887. He never did get the trial Rome had ordered. And his priest friends, especially Father O'Callaghan, *noticed this*. They used his funeral to show their hurt by demanding that the bishop say the Mass. He did say the Mass; but in the sacristy beforehand, O'Callaghan told the bishop that it was Father Quinn's wish that no sermon be given at that Mass. In a way, this was the ultimate in loyal opposition.

In August 1884, Bishop Gilmour went to Bellevue, Ohio, to dedicate a new church there. Father O'Callaghan was one of many priests invited to the affair. Conversation that took place on this occasion gave rise to an exchange of letters between these two men which, while it was very harsh, was productive of a real friendship between them in the end. The correspondence began when Gilmour wrote O'Callaghan on August 20, 1884:

At my last visit to Bellevue, you took considerable pains to advance in my presence and in the presence of others, a number of propositions highly offensive to Catholic morality, fact, and law; and if they were maintained, they would unhinge respect for the Church and her mission. Among these were the following:

1) The conditional possibility of the Pope teaching heresy.
2) The Church was a 'trimmer.'
3) You and the others applauding assent to the scandal-

ous and false proposition of Reverend Smith 'That all the evil in the Church comes from Bishops.'

4) That infirm priests have a right *ex justitia* for support.

5) That the Church in America is not a missionary Church and priests in America are not missionary priests.

The *first* proposition is heretical. The *second* is an attack on the Church containing the essence of all the accusations against the policy of the Church from Voltaire to Renan. The *third* is false and scandalous and tends to bring the episcopacy into contempt.

The *fourth* is against law, ignorance of which you cannot plead since I published it as part of the law governing the Infirm Priests' Fund.

The *fifth* is also against fact and law and was advanced by you in the spirit of the rising radicalism of a wing of the clergy in this country.

. . . These ideas are not only held by you but are a part of your daily thought and teaching. I am glad and sorry that they were uttered; glad to know your teachings; sorry that such teachings are found among priests of this diocese . . . You will let me know how far you maintain such doctrines that I may know what to do in this matter.

Here was a challenge by the bishop to the faith of one of his priests. O'Callaghan replied tersely and with precision on August 24, 1884:

I hasten to reply . . . and begin by denying that the five propositions you quote are *mine* except the *second* and *fourth*. I acknowledge the term 'trimmer' applied to the Church is an offensive and scandalous term which I regretted at the moment and do now regret . . . I retracted it immediately as you must remember . . . The idea I wished to convey is correct however, viz., that the Church sometimes conforms to the usurping demands of the State and under restraint, allows the State rights which properly belong to her. Witness the nomination of bishops by kings, the various concordats, etc. . . I acknowledge the *fourth proposition,* it is not mine as you limit it . . . There was no allusion to infirm priests of this diocese and therefore none to your 'law'. . . I spoke in general of infirm missionary priests in the United States. Evidently you desire my reason. Well, then, I believe that an infirm missionary priest is by the Natural, Divine, Positive and Ecclesiastical Law entitled to his support, whether *in justitia* or *in congruo* matters little.

. . . There is no law forbidding me to hold this position . . . You impose a *tax* to be paid at a specific time to support infirm priests. You charge interest or arrears of this *tax.* Does it look like simple volunteer charity? You know I have observed this law to the letter, and holding this opinion makes me more exact in fulfilling it.

The *fifth proposition* is not mine as you state it. I said the Church in America in many places was losing its missionary character and approaching a fixed status . . . You yourself, Rt. Reverend Bishop said as much about many dioceses in the East . . . I did not say 'the priests are not missionary priests.' *I know they are such* and will continue until the status is changed by law. I said priests had a right to petition for a change in status. You objected to the term *'right.'* Why even slaves have the right to petition . . .

The other propositions are not mine. But as you desire to know how far they are held by me, I will frankly inform you. I confess I did not know that the first proposition as stated by you was heretical until your letter informed me.

I do believe the Pope teaching *'ex cathedra'* is infallible. I needed no definition of the Vatican Council to cause my assent to this; I have always so believed. But I thought I was not obliged *de fide* to believe that the Pope as a private theologian or in private conversation or in instructing an individual is infallible . . . . I think all theologians of note hold this distinction. Lately it has been developed by Cardinal Newman in his several replies to Gladstone.

If I laughed at the *third proposition* it was at the sweeping absurdity of the charge.

I have now given my answer to your five propositions. May I say, in passing, that one should be very careful in stating, after the lapse of some time, the propositions of another. . . Is it logical or charitable to conclude that because a priest holds certain opinions, they become his daily teaching? . . . Charity thinks no evil.

I have now given you my judgment *in extenso* and without reservation upon these five propositions . . . I thank you for your interest in my orthodoxy and I pray that neither in this diocese, nor in any other, may there be any false teaching. I solemnly declare that I hold and believe from my whole heart all the truths the Holy Catholic Church teaches . . . If I have sinned ever, it has been, as you know, by being an ultra, ultra montane.

This should have ended whatever it was that was disturbing the bishop. But he was not satisfied. He seems to have desired a simple and full retraction of the five propositions, as he stated them. Gilmour was back again writing O'Callaghan on August 29, 1884:

Your and my propositions were about the Pope — not about a private theologian — hence your disquisition is not *ad rem.* Your regret of the word 'trimmer' came from be-

ing corrected. Your assertion that the Church in America
is not missionary leaves you as the author of this statement . . . Now I wish to correct you, not so much on your
contra-legem teaching but on the . . . unsound doctrines you
utter. Had you and your confreres' utterances at Bellevue
been the extravagances of thoughtlessness they could have
been excused. But they are clearly the habitual doctrines
of your 'wing' that had long and often been discussed among
you . . . .

When men assail bishops and law, they generally end
up with disrespect for both. The right to respectfully discuss laws and men must be conceded and maintained; also
the right of petition, which I never denied. The obligation
of a diocese to care for its sick priests must be urged; but
the title by which we were ordained (missionaries) must be
accepted. Had this not been so violently denied, we would
have more peace and concord — *and less Roman interference.*

Let us discuss; but cease assailing bishops . . . You and
your confreres should be less wild and scandalous than you
were at Bellevue. . . . I admonish you of the current you
are in.

Here Bishop Gilmour was trying to say something about
the Sunday night meetings of priests at O'Callaghan's rectory.
He hints at something conspiratorial, and this, plus a number
of similar innuendoes voiced by the bishop over a period of
years, appears to have pushed O'Callaghan beyond his usual
reticence. When he addressed the bishop on personal matters,
he seems to have been quite open and candid. But when he was
prodded to speak for many, O'Callaghan, for the first time with
Bishop Gilmour, writes from both a position of defense and

offense. In the longest letter he will ever write to a bishop, on September 3, 1884, he begins by stressing his personal integrity:

I have received your letter of the 29th of August surcharged with a new series of accusations and invectives . . . Your letter compels me, against my desire, not to be silent, for my silence might, by you, be distorted into an admission of the truth and justice of them, and thus be taken as proof of my guilt. I shall therefore reply at length and freely, nevertheless, I hope, with due respect. In defending myself, I can scarcely escape at times, offending you, at least in your opinion, especially when I see how bitterly and even violently you write to me. But if I shall be accused of this new offense it may be as much owing to your readiness to find fault where none may exist, as to my neglectfulness of reverence. You still hold me the 'author' of four of the five of those propositions . . . The burden of proof rests with you. If you wish, summon witnesses, but until then, repeat those charges no more . . .

You said in your last letter 'you took considerable pains to advance in my presence and in the presence of others a number of propositions highly offensive, etc.' If I took such 'considerable pains' to 'advance,' . . . others as well as you would remember this. Much as I regard your memory and veracity, I prefer to be convinced as between you and me, by my own habit of thought, and I do know that your presentation of these propositions is absolutely foreign to it. No one ever heard me advance such propositions. What might help convince you that you are mistaken is the fact that while I deny that I am the 'author' of these propositions, I will defend them; the worst of them absolutely, the others when slightly modified. What motive could I have in denying that I asserted them? I would far rather have your rebuke and discipline for any rash, ignorant, or extravagant utterance, than escape with your contempt, in knowing me to be a willful and craven liar.

With this introduction completed, O'Callaghan then turns to three of the five propositions the bishop had accused him of authoring. These he says he did not author, but will defend. He said:

> You, Rt. Rev. Bishop, have accused me of holding a heretical opinion, and farther on you reach the climax of your arraignment when you charge this, as well as many other bad things, has been my 'daily thought and teaching.' Do you take it as a trifling matter to brand a priest as a malicious, persistent and active heretic? Do you think I have no feeling; no sense of honor; no conscience; no duty to Religion; that I should tamely submit to this outrage especially coming from my bishop?
>
> . . . I will not be silent, I will defend myself . . . Here is, in your own words, the proposition which you call heretical; 'the conditional possibility of the Pope teaching heresy.' It is not a complete proposition, but it is intelligible. You say this is heretical; I say no . . . If in private audience, (as you said happened to you), the Pope told you something that touched on morals or doctrine, is it heresy to say he might possibly err? You say yes; I say no, and all theologians are with me . . . I shall quote an authority who cannot be suspected of Gallicanism, Cardinal Newman. In his book on the Vatican Council, p. 140, he says: 'The Vatican Council has determined that the Pope is infallible only when he speaks *ex cathedra'*. . . I refer you again to Cardinal Newman's letter to the Duke of Norfolk on Gladstone's Expostulation, p. 160 to p. 164, where you will find matters of 'fact and law' and where you will see your

strange condemnation is not in accord with either fact or law . . . .

O'Callaghan then went into a lengthy treatment of whether many parishes in the United States were not already permanent and not missionary. Then he examined the rights of infirm priests to receive support from their diocese in justice, repeating almost word for word, arguments which he had written fifteen years earlier, in the Jus Letters. Finally, O'Callaghan ended his letter with these comments on the style of the bishop which in the end seem to have won him Gilmour's respect. He challenged the bishop's conscience:

> Consider Rt. Rev. Bishop, the tone and burden of your letter; not only these last, but former ones, and ask yourself in all conscience, are these reproaches and epithets merited; 'conspiracies,' 'cabals,' 'cliques,' 'wings,' 'rings,' 'rebels,' 'radicals,' 'discords,' 'disobedience,' 'false-teachings,' 'unsound doctrines,' and now 'heretics'! I could fill a page with these opprobrious epithets. It requires more than human patience to continue to submit to these invectives, and heroic zeal to labor sedulously while they are poured out upon priests without cause and without measure. These are not only written, but repeated in your talk, to the injury of the good name of the priests of your diocese. One might naturally suppose that this was done through vanity to show what a great man you are to be able to govern such a set of rascals. But in all sincerity, I believe it to be rather the result of a fervid imagination begetting illusions, rather than sober judgments. And under the influence of these delusions, you honestly express what you so erroneously believe to be your grievances. In this way, I can excuse you from the sin of calumny, but nevertheless, your priests are the sufferers. Rt. Rev. Bishop, do heretics work as hard

as I and my confreres do? Are conspirators so frank and outspoken? How long does it take for a conspiracy to hatch? The one against you must be more than thirteen years incubating, and yet it shows no sign of life.

Gilmour had been thirteen years bishop of Cleveland in 1884. O'Callaghan was telling him that the fact that priests noticed what they thought was his misuse of power on occasion in no way implied they were conspiring against him. O'Callaghan went on:

The dangers that surround you are like those that threaten a man in the delirium of fever. Lately, on the 25th anniversary of my ordination I left the city purposely to escape any demonstration however limited or innocent because I knew your prejudices and feared the exciting of your suspicions. Had these prejudices not existed, what was said that summer afternoon in Bellevue might have passed for a very innocent affair . . . I can say now that my motive and intentions in Bellevue were of the kindest nature no matter how sadly I failed in manifesting them. I saw you sitting alone in that room. I approached you after urging all the other priests to do likewise, to entertain you and help you pass a pleasant hour with many priests you do not really know, and who do not really know you . . . . But while intending to please you, I only gave offense. In a few years, dear Bishop, we will all have passed away and few will remember us either in praise or prayer. Is there not enough to engage us, each in his respective sphere, without these acerbities to annoy us? God will judge us all; and He will reverse many judgments men have made. I pray that both you and I will receive His favorable judgment.

Gilmour had asked, in the letter that called forth this outpouring from O'Callaghan, "Let us discuss." Here, O'Callaghan had truly opened himself, one suspects not without some difficulty. Gilmour's reply on September 20, 1884, notes this. The bishop begins:

> I am glad for this correspondence. It has cleared the whole atmosphere and will, I hope, bring about better understanding where there should be brotherly love and ministerial sympathy.

Now, for the first time, Bishop Gilmour accepted Father O'Callaghan's friendship. This friendship would be tested; (Father John Quinn was still sick in the Toledo hospital) but it would last firmly until Gilmour's death in April 1891.

The bishop's letter went on to say:

> If you had discussed these questions this way in Bellevue, you and I would fully agree in principle, and much in detail... I misunderstood you altogether in Bellevue, and I must say I am glad I did, because now we have spoken truly, man to man... At no time did I ever dream you were heretical — that requires contumacy — nor did I ever think that guarded in your language, you would utter words that would have the appearance of unorthodoxy... If we jarred each other, the jarring has quickened and purified us....

By admitting misunderstanding Gilmour had given something of himself away, no easy thing for a man more than sixty years old, or in his position. Now he would complain about an attitude he felt he was meeting in O'Callaghan and his friends;

> You wrote a number of descriptive words I had used... Had you and some of those who follow you given me, or would you give me now, the loyal supporting assistance that your great talents and virtues could give, these words would

never be needed ... Negative loyalty is not much, and that is the best and the most that I usually receive from you ... Has this ever hindered me from placing you or your friends in places of responsibility, even when I thought you were working against me?

Again, it would seem that Gilmour did not quite grasp the fact that O'Callaghan's dissent was not personal; nor does he seem to see the need for loyal opposition which, it appears, he read as "negative loyalty."

However, he goes on to open himself further to O'Callaghan at a level of humility which must have been very difficult, and which reveals a certain sadness and loneliness which must always exist at the top of any structure. He wrote:

From the beginning, I have, by circumstances, been forced into a position and into the assertion of a character which I do not now enjoy, and which I have for a long time regretted. My desire is to be an active cooperator with the priests in their love and brotherly association. I have got these things reluctantly, and so I have been forced back upon myself, and I have appeared cold, resistive and unsympathetic. You and your friends meet regularly. You discuss ideas, and you do not invite me to join you. You have treated me as a stranger in your midst .... I must not be forced to assert forever that I am the bishop as we do together, ordinary, routine work ... I must not be forced to rule by authority instead of persuasion. All the give must not be on one side only.

From this time on, the bishop was invited to the Sunday night buffet dinners at O'Callaghan's rectory. Only twice, however, did he attend. One wonders why. One also might wonder whether O'Callaghan ever showed this very warm letter from the bishop to any of his priest friends.

Probably not. It would have been a violation of his sense of role as leader of the opposition, and his sense of conscience in guarding private confidences.

In any case, it would be naive to say that after this exchange, either man failed to continue his outspokenness as they addressed each other in the years left for them both. But their letters to one another are warmer, more courteous and lacking altogether any note of mistrust.

An exchange of this sort occurred in 1889. In May of that year, Gilmour asked the pastors of Cleveland city parishes to help one evening in hearing confessions at the City Workhouse, a trustee farm for petty criminals. He said ruefully:

All pastors have parishioners in this institution.

O'Callaghan had a quasi-assistant at this time, an old friend, who had a problem with alcohol. The bishop had sent this man to live with O'Callaghan, hoping that their friendship would preserve the assistant's sobriety. O'Callaghan sent the assistant to hear the Workhouse confessions. Gilmour discovered this fact, and on June 2, 1889, he wrote O'Callaghan:

I wrote you asking that you personally go to the Workhouse to help hear confessions of the prisoners, some of whom are from your parish. But you sent your assistant! For this, I wonder that you did not go yourself. But to send a priest there who is as your assistant is beyond wonder. Please keep your assistant at St. Colman's. To prevent further doubt, I hereby confine his faculties to St. Colman's.

O'Callaghan answered on June 16, 1889:

I received yours of the 2nd blaming me for not going to hear confessions at the Workhouse. I did not for some time think your letter required an answer, but on consideration, I think an answer is due you.

I wish, Rt. Rev. Bishop, to remove from your mind any idea that I meant to disregard your request for I assure you I never had such a thought; I did not think the request was that I go personally, so I asked the assistant and he went. He was not at all to blame. If any blame is due, it is due to me but as I said, I had no idea of meriting blame.

My motive for this writing is to ease your mind and remove from it any notion that I would deliberately disregard your request. I believe you have enough to trouble you without my contributing my share.

What he is also saying is that the bishop should not punish this assistant too harshly; if Gilmour wants to punish anyone, let it be O'Callaghan. That assistant must have been strengthened by O'Callaghan's presence. He put in eight good years at St. Colman's until his death in 1896.

The "enough trouble" Gilmour had, refers, without doubt, to a suit the bishop had instigated in civil court in Toledo. Gilmour had adopted a policy of allowing priests who were ordained elsewhere and who applied to work in the Cleveland diocese, to serve congregations in the diocese for a period just under five years. Then, before such priests would receive incardination, the bishop would revoke their faculties and tell them to move on.

One such priest was Father John B. Primeau who had come to the Cleveland diocese in 1883. Gilmour appointed him pastor of St. Louis parish, Toledo. In 1888, Primeau received the usual notification that his faculties would cease on December 16 and that as of that date, he was no longer a Cleveland priest.

Primeau appealed to the Archbishop of Cincinnati and

refused to vacate the rectory in which he lived. Gilmour took quick action; he sought from a Toledo Magistrate's Court an eviction proceeding. Primeau appealed against this eviction to the Court of Common Pleas in Toledo, and the bishop found himself involved in a public trial against one of his priests.

The trial lasted from March 20 until May 10, 1889. It received wide publicity; the bishop was put on the stand for days at a time. One such day was Holy Thursday of that year when no oils were consecrated in the diocese. Moreover, he lost the case. It was finally settled in an ecclesiastical court in Cincinnati where Primeau had had recourse in the first place.

Bishop Gilmour kept a diary and the entry for March 18, 1889, two days before the trial was to begin, notes that he had a visit from Father O'Callaghan, who "in a highly persuasive way urged me to drop the suit in the Toledo court against Reverend Primeau. I refused. I will have law and order, come what may."

O'Callaghan's letter on the Workhouse confession issue does not miss the opportunity to tell the bishop that the "trouble" he has could have been avoided if the bishop had listened to one of his priests who foresaw the danger and scandal involved in such a situation. It also says more; here was loyal opposition in the form of a plea from one of his priests, who had not missed chances in the past to challenge the bishop in Ecclesiastical Courts, seeking due process there. But O'Callaghan, recalling what he had learned from Judge Thomas Stanfield while a student at Notre Dame, forty years earlier, knew that the due process he prayed for was to be found in the Canons of the Church, not in civil court.

He also seems to have known that his bishop, or worse, the Church, somehow would be beaten, even if the civil verdict had been different. But beating the bishop surely was not O'Callaghan's goal.

VIII

It would be no exaggeration to say that the vast majority of the priests and bishops living in the United States at the time of the Vatican Council of 1870 were familiar with the thought of Father Eugene O'Callaghan. This thought was developed in a systematic series of anonymous letters published in *The New York Freeman's Journal* between December 1868 and March 1870. The letters were signed simply "Jus," and came to be known as the "Jus Letters."

In the decade which preceded Vatican I, *The Freeman's Journal* was the most widely read Catholic newspaper in this country. It was operated and edited by James A. McMaster, a New England Yankee, who was converted to the Catholic Church in 1844. Unlike the other Catholic weekly newspapers of that period, *The Freeman's Journal* was not the official organ of any bishop or diocese. Like the *Harper's Weekly* which it imitated in many ways, *The Freeman's Journal* had a national scope, concentrating its feature stories on Church news in various parts of the United States and by telegraph on Europe also.

More than 85% of the English-speaking diocesan clergy of the United States subscribed to *The Freeman's Journal* in the 1860's. It was to this clerical audience especially that the Jus Letters were directed. The Letters generally ran about 2500 words; there were twelve in all, and they were titled "The Status of the Clergy in America."

There was a real urgency to the subject. In 1866, the Bishops of the United States had met in Plenary Session at Baltimore and petitioned Rome to continue the "missionary" status of this country "for twenty years or perhaps forever." There had been no report made back to the priests of any diocese by any bishop of this action and so it was not until the *Acts of the Second Plenary Council of Baltimore* was published late in 1867 (in Latin) that the clergy of America became aware of what their bishops had done.

A groundswell feeling of resentment began to mount quickly. This was finally articulated, in language both theoretical and pastoral, by O'Callaghan in the Jus Letters. The sense of urgency was accentuated by the general excitement which preceded the convocation of the 20th Ecumenical Council of the Universal Church by Pope Pius IX on December 8, 1869.

O'Callaghan urged the secular (diocesan) priests of the United States to bring their grievances to the attention of the Council. The early Jus Letters described these grievances and the need for a change in the status of the Church in America. Timing his first letter exactly a year before the Council was to open, O'Callaghan began by discussing conservatism. On December 12, 1868, he wrote:

> It is usual for a certain class of meticulous persons, whether in Church or State, to feel alarm if anyone, no matter how cogent the reasons, would advocate a change in the existing state of things. These happy souls, always content with the present, no matter how imperfect, never consider the future, and are ever ready to denounce the idea of change, no matter how productive of good or how easily affected because forsooth 'It betrays a discontented spirit.' But these good souls never reflect that even discontentment may be a virtue when, dissatisfied with a less perfect state of things, it endeavors by a *legitimate* means to substitute a better system . . . They call themselves *conservatives* and scout the idea of change, but they should remember that

while conservatism is a very praiseworthy quality, it may be abused. The Scribes and Pharisees of old were conservatives and would not tolerate a change, even by the introduction of a perfect law, to supersede an imperfect and preparatory law. Yet they erred. And may it not happen that the *conservatives* of today err who oppose the introduction of Canon Law to supply the place of the imperfect and preparatory law of the Missionary System? The relation of Missionary Law to Canon Law may not inaptly be compared to the relations existing between the old law and the new law, the latter being in each case the perfection and fulfillment of the former. If conservatives then, are content with the present state of things, they cannot surely blame us if, like the prophets and saints of old, we look forward and sigh for a better state and cry out 'How long, O Lord, how long?' And as the seventy weeks of years were shortened because of the desire of the children of God, who knows but that the twenty years of Mission life petitioned for by our Most Reverend and Right Reverend Prelates may be shortened by our sighs and desires.

Conservatism, if regulated is good; its idea has been implanted in the heart of man, and without it, there could be no order, no permanence, no society. But like all gifts of God conservatism may be grossly abused; like other passions it may be abused by excess as well as defect. By defect, it runs into anarchy and revolution; by excess it dwindles into old-fogyism and fossility. If the advocates of the former would rush the world into chaos, the advocates of the latter are not less its enemies, for they would clog the wheels of progress and bring the world to a dead halt by their theory of optimism.

Many are *conservatives* in the vicious sense from *want of reflection;* some from *inertia,* some from want of *prin-*

ciple who will do nothing unless *self* is the immediate motive; others again from *timidity,* for no one can advocate a change without being suspected by the indifferent, and more or less persecuted by those in whose interest it is to preserve present status. Of course it is natural for the favored few, whether Church or State, always to advocate the continuance of the existing system, and prove themselves uncompromising conservatives . . . .

I am of the opinion that the Missionary state of Church discipline should generally cease among us and give place to the government of Church Law. American Protestants and even American Catholic laymen have scarcely a conception of the beauty and grandeur of *Catholic* discipline in its full and perfect development. Intelligent and liberty-loving Protestants would then admire the wisdom and equity of her laws, as they now admire the beauty and sublimity of her music, her painting, her sculpture, and her architecture . . .

How much greater influence would not her salutary law have upon the practical and liberty-loving American mind. Painting, music, etc., belong more to the ideal, but law and right are practical matter-of-fact things, just such as would seize the attention of our Protestant brethren, and present before them the true spirit of the Church in her external operations. Every American should then, admire the justice of the Church, her hatred of oppression, her protection of the weak against the strong; he should confess that her canons are the *beau ideal* of order and true liberty. Is it wrong for us respectfully and submissively to ask why this may not supersede our existing, imperfect, and in many instances, unavoidably oppressive and odious Missionary system? It's certain that the missionary state is the infant state, the undeveloped state of Church discipline.

It exists not from choice but from necessity, being barely *tolerated* until circumstances permit its partial or entire discontinuance. But the Church in America is no longer in its infant state; its old well-established hierarchy forbids this notion; its numerous and flourishing churches, universities, colleges and religious houses forbid the notion. In the presence then of such a state of things, to retain the Missionary discipline of the Church is like wrapping a full-grown man in swaddling clothes and feeding him on pap. 'When I was a child,' says St. Paul, 'I spoke as a child, I understood as a child, I thought as a child, but when I became a man I put away the things of a child.'

If there is anyone unaware that our present system of discipline is not that preferred by Rome, in order to be undeceived he has only to pay attention to two considerations. *First consideration*: the Prelates of the United States, assembled in council at Baltimore in 1866, *petitioned* the Holy Father to permit the Missionary status of the Church to continue for twenty years more in America. From this it follows that Rome *suffers* the Missionary condition to continue only by *toleration* as a necessary evil, as a lesser good. *Second consideration*: but Rome *refused to grant* this petition which plainly shows that Rome desires the cessation of the Missionary state among us, either immediately or very soon; it urges upon our Prelates the necessity of substituting a government of law for a government of *arbitrary* character, in a word, the government of an infallible and divine Church instead of the government of one or a few bishops having no title to infallibility, no matter how great their virtue or wisdom. Now is it disrespectful, is it rash, is it 'imprudent' for us to 'petition' our bishops to conform to the wishes of Rome and introduce parishes and government by the canons? Shall we be called discontent spirits, etc.? If so, we are only discontented as to what Rome barely tolerates . . .

Again there is another consideration that intimately concerns the laity as to why the Missionary system should cease. One of the principal duties of the pastor is to offer up the Adorable Sacrifice for his people. Every pastor is obliged in justice as well as in charity to do this every Sunday and holy day for the benefit of his congregation. But at present no priest is *obliged* to do so, for Rome has decided that a missionary priest is obliged neither by justice nor charity to discharge this important office since he is not properly a pastor. Of course, every priest having charge of a congregation will of his own charitable impulse give them this opportunity of treasuring up graces drawn from the Holy Sacrifice; but if they had a pastor, if they were regarded as a Parish, then they would be entitled to it and could demand it as a right.

On February 6, 1869, O'Callaghan published the second Jus Letter. Its main theme was that American priests under the missionary system lacked security and that this lack of security was detrimental to the interests of the spirit of Religion among Catholics in America. The insecurity of the priest he sees as a double danger. The continuous transferring of priests without warning or consultation he saw as demoralizing to the clergy. Moreover, O'Callaghan said it debilitated congregations which were living at peace with their pastor and with their bishop. He began with an analogy:

As the fragrance of the rose pervades the whole garden, so the spirit of the Catholic Church diffuses itself through the fields of her operations. Hence she communicates to all things connected with her service the idea of permanence and perpetuity. Even the very materials of which her

Church edifices are composed when the Church is consecrated are dedicated to God forever and cannot without profanation be diverted to secular uses. She abhors change and alteration and yields even in things essentially changeable (as matters of discipline) only when necessity and the good of religion demand it, for she is the spouse of 'Jesus Christ yesterday, today, and *the same forever,* with whom there is no change or shadow of vicissitude.' The spirit of her laws and ordinances is to carry out the will of our Savior as expressed in the Lord's Prayer: 'thy Kingdom come; thy will be done on earth *as it is in Heaven*' — where there is no changing, no rewards without merit, and certainly no depredation without cause.

Is it to be wondered then that the laws of the Church, where fully and freely administered, constitute the parish priest inamovable, clothe him for jurisdiction independent of the bishop, make his removal impossible, unless for specific causes and *then* not at the nod of the bishop, but after a fair and impartial trial by the issue of which the bishop himself is as much obligated as the priest?

Let us for a moment scrutinize the wisdom of the Church Missionary establishing her pastors *inamovable.* We may therefore ask what good can come from changing a priest from congregation to congregation as if they were some sort of quack doctors . . .

Let us therefore suppose an American bishop. To advocate the necessity of this frequent removal and in order to strengthen this cause we will suppose the gravest objections.

Bishop: A priest may be unworthy of the ministry and should be removed from his charge.

Answer: Granted most readily — aye, even he should not receive another until he has given indubitable proof of a sincere repentance. But is this a reason why a worthy pastor should be removed? Is this a reason why we should not have regularly established parish priests with the right of inamovability? The canons sufficiently provide for the case objected to, and even such a one where a parish priest has *jus inamovibilitatis* would not prevent his removal.

Bishop: Another congregation may need the services of a certain priest; a bishop ought to have the power to remove him at will.

Answer: If this removal is for the reward of the priest and *he is willing,* then the bishop may propose and the priest will *accept.* Otherwise I deny the propriety of compulsory removal. If the removal be a favor then it implies the option on the part of the priest to refuse for you *cannot compel* a man to accept a favor; if so it is no longer a favor but a yoke. But if this removal implies a degradation — as is always the case when a priest is involuntarily changed from a better to a worse congregation —the Church will not approve of such indignities. She will not permit her ministers to be deprived without a crime, and recent appeals to Rome, if I am rightly informed, prove that even the absolutism of American bishops will not justify them before Rome in the arbitrary degrading of a priest.

Bishop: But he can do more good elsewhere.

Answer: Even if so, he is not obligated in conscience *per se* to leave a congregation in which he is doing good and is loved even to do more good elsewhere. How many priests in Catholic countries could be spared to the Foreign Missions to labor in savage lands for the salvation of the untaught? Yet none would think of accusing such priests of sin because they do not go. Some American bishops would do a great deal of good in China or Africa, as Vicars Apostolic or as simple priests, but they do not go and I suppose they do not accuse themselves of sin because they neglect to do all the good they might do. Therefore, if a priest is doing good work, is contented where he is, and especially if he is liked by his flock, a bishop should not remove him on the plea that he may do more good in another congregation.

Bishop: There is a church to be built in a certain congregation and a certain priest is prudent, zealous and a good financier with all. Therefore it is right to remove him.

Answer: Because a priest possesses these praiseworthy qualities, is it a reason why he should be dragged from a congregation in which he for years was obliged to strain these qualities in building and paying for a church, a school house, a residence, etc., in order to make room for some episcopal favorite who may be too inert to do these things for himself? In any case why should this good priest be compelled to repeat some labors over again as soon as they are completed? Is this justice?

Bishop: A priest may be disliked by his congregation, therefore the bishop should have the right to remove indiscriminately.

Answer: Try him by the canons; if he is guilty, remove him; if not, why should he be punished because of the clamors of the people unless, as Pilate did to Christ, you crucify him without cause to please the people. Such yielding to the unjust demands of a congregation must be productive only to their spiritual ruin.

Bishop: I dislike this priest for personal reasons and desire to punish him by removing him.

Answer: This is the plea of a tyrant, not of a bishop. The Church does not permit this. You approve her spirit and prevent her general laws from coming into operation in order to indulge your personal piques, your sympathies and antipathies. This is neither Christian nor manly . . .

I have alluded to a congregation wishing to get rid of its pastor, but this is so rare in the Catholic Church as to merit no further notice. On the contrary, we have frequent instances of congregations weeping and sobbing to a man on their pastor being torn from them by their bishop and petitioning in vain for his return. We have even many instances of congregations going into almost open schism for this very reason and afterwards, requiring many years of careful nursing to reconcile them. Even this nursing will always prove useless in some individual cases and there will always remain behind enough of the old leaven to make the ministry of the successor of such a pastor anything but pleasant. Can good come out of this? Can religion be advanced by severing those ties of affection so necessary to the good government of a people? Do not tell me a pastor must be indifferent and callous toward his flock and repel in his people any other than manifestation of the same feelings toward himself. Heaven forbid such a condition! Unless, of course, we reverse the gospel idea of the 'good pastor' and the 'mercenary.' The affection of a congregation is the most powerful lever a pastor can use in directing and ministering to them . . .

The family is the true type of union of flock and pastor. Even the names of father and children used reciprocally by the flock and their pastor in their daily intercourse indicate the close, affectionate and enduring union that shall exist between them. The pastor is truly the father to his flock for he more than guarantees them, he regenerates them. He gives them a spiritual birth and endows them with a spiritual birthright through his ministry, he provides for their daily wants by breaking for them the bread of life. The spirit of the Church is that these spiritual ties should be as strong and enduring as possible and that nothing should be done to weaken or disrupt them. Yet our present system, just as divorce in the natural family, breaks up these spiritual relations and the evils that frequently ensue thereupon prove the wisdom of the Church; in making the union of a pastor with his flock permanent her wisdom is also manifest in making the union of the family indissoluble.

The lack of any responsibility on the part of American bishops in justice toward aged or infirm priests O'Callaghan saw as the second source of insecurity and a great potential danger to the building of the American Church. This is the theme he develops in a letter published three weeks later which began with another analogy, this one, quite personal, coming from a man who found himself forever separated from his own native land and trying to become a full citizen of an adopted land.

God has imparted in the heart of every man a love of locality, and adaptability to surrounding circumstances and an attachment to those scenes in which he has labored, even for a few years. The existence of this feeling cannot be denied: it is *cognate to the love of our native land* and is necessary in the divine economy to render men contented and happy in localities naturally inhospitable and dreary. Where there is not some mysterious attraction of this kind, places naturally barren and uninviting but now smiling under the careful attention of the husbandman, would have been bleak deserts, abandoned by all for places more blessed by nature. Behold the wisdom of God in thus constructing man in the natural order so as to effect this great end. To this cause in the natural order, but more especially to *grace in the supernatural order is it due that almost every priest is content with his position,* with his congregation and his congregation satisfied with him. What good can come then to changing, supposing that a priest is doing well where he is? It is contrary to the law of nature, contrary to the spirit of the Church, contrary to the will of the priest, contrary to the will of the people, contrary to prudence and good sense, and contrary to the interests of religion.

But let us view this question in another light. A priest finds himself in a large congregation with a rickety old church into which the people must be wedged each Sunday. He finds there is need for a church, a cemetery, a schoolhouse, a residence, etc. Like a prudent builder, he calculates his means, weighs the circumstances that may affect him in the accomplishment of his intention. Before he proceeds far in theorizing, he finds that half a dozen hard facts stare him in the face; no imaginations, but stern actual realities which like Banquo's ghost, will not be put down, even at the voice of zeal.

1st fact. His bishop offers him a paltry salary, in some dioceses not so much as may be earned by a common laboring man.

2nd fact. He knows from experience that as soon as he begins to build his church, *perequisitions will dwindle to almost nothing,* his people generally can afford to give but a certain amount, and being obliged to give that to the church, there remains nothing for the priest.

3rd fact. In order to stimulate his people to liberality, *he must show the example himself* and therefore he must contribute of his indigence as much as his flock gives of their competence.

4th fact. While the channels of his emoluments are dried up, his labors are doubled and tripled frequently, so much so as to exhaust all his energies and *break down his health* and make him invalid during the rest of his life.

5th fact. Supposing that all his work is accomplished and all his debts are liquidated, at the very time when *after years of toil and privation he should expect a little rest in the enjoyment of the fruits of his labors, he receives an episcopal edict ordering him presto to some Siberia in the diocese* where he might meditate on the folly of a priest's expectation under the present system of discipline.

6th fact. Even if a priest be not removed from the field of his great labor and trials after conquering them the *bishop can hold the fear of removal* over him like a rod and whip him into servility and sycophancy.

7th fact. He knows that in case of old age or infirmity, even though that infirmity be induced in the heroic discharge of his duties, *he is under the present system entitled in justice to no support whatever.* He cannot claim as a right even a bite of bread. The late Council is far from being vague or obscure on this point for it distinctly informs the priest that *he can claim nothing as a right.* If he be infirm, he is entitled to nothing by justice and that even if there should be established a fund for infirm priests, unless he contributed to it, he should, in case of age or infirmity, be entitled to nothing. He has no right to claim his support from the bishop to whom he belonged or from the people in whose service he spent himself.

Some of your lay readers may be shocked by these considerations, but I beg to tell them that this is no fancy or predawn figure. *I have seen these things happen to my fellow priests.* These are the logical consequences of the present system which I am discussing in its merits. It is true that some religious communities or some pious Catholic layman may afford the poor infirm or aged priest an asylum from motives of charity, but the logical consequence remains, he has no right in justice unless it be the right to die a pauper.

Is it then becoming to the dignity of priesthood, is it the due to the zeal and the sacrifices of the clergy that even such possibilities should be concluded logically from the present abnormal status of the Catholic clergy in the U.S.? I could add a dozen other facts if space and prudence permitted. But enough.

In the face of these facts, with what heart can a priest begin to work? Will he burden himself with labors only to cut off his prerequisites, exhaust his strength, ruin his health, expose himself as a victim of arbitrary rule; *absolutism with no right to depend on* but the right of a pauper guaranteed by the state? Will he not rather let the school, cemetery, etc., to shift for themselves, *live at ease,* hoard up his prerequisites and do nothing to retard their income; in a word, *he will act the mercenary* and extort all he can from his flock for they are not his flock and he is not their pastor. Thus he will *make a traffic of the ministry* under the laudable pretense of providing for himself against the days of age or infirmity since the present system denies him every right and leaves him to starve when no longer able to labor. Even the slave system guaranteed certain rights to aged and infirm slaves; they could not be left to starve or to live on the charity of the benevolent. *Yet such is our present ecclesiastical policy in America in the year of grace,* 1869.

Is such a system calculated to free them from the anxiety and worldly solicitude that tends to cool the ardor and abate the energy of the minister of God?

Our bishops, in council and out of it *complain of the insufficient numbers of young men who prepare themselves for the ministry.* They complain of the want of vocations. Perhaps if they reflected, they would see that the cause is want of encouragement. *What father, in the face of these facts would educate his son at great expense for a state in which he is protected not by a single law and enjoys not a single right* to save him from the possible injunction of his bishop? What young man, knowing these facts even if urged by his father, would consent to expose himself to such a condition of things? No wonder then that vocations are few and that *thousands in America are lost for want of priests to minister to them.*

The priests of America have proved themselves in zeal and disinterestedness second to no clergy in the world. They have labored under a system that paralyzes their efforts and blunts every stimulus and zeal; they have labored under the most adverse circumstances to build up religion in America while every motive of prudence and self-preservation prompted them to a different course. *Were our priests not unselfish, nay heroic, they would be rich and the Church in America poor;* poor in churches; poor in schools, etc. etc.; but on the contrary, our churches and schools are comparatively rich and prosperous while *our priests are very very poor. All honor to the priests of America.* I cannot say all honor to a *system that tempts* them to a different career and, like Judas to betray their master for wealth.

Our Savior intimated this when He said that when we see the signs of the times it is prudent to prepare for them.

But it is said that some bishops seldom or never exercise their power. All honor to their wisdom. May their number rapidly increase. It was said that some slavemasters never disturbed or sold their slaves. This was humane. But when it was answered that death or accident might deprive these slaves of their masters, where then was their happiness, their protection? May it not be so with those good bishops and their happy priests? I would use a different illustration if it came to me, but I confess in humiliation that I could find none more appropos.

The priests of America must take speedy action unless they wish to remain in their present unprotected position for twenty and perhaps, for fifty years to come. Opportunities do not every year present themselves. *The present is our golden opportunity.* Shall we let it pass? While Providence spares Pius IX, the great reformer of the Church, let us take prompt, speedy and decisive action. *Let us pray him to turn a benignant eye toward America, the land of promise for the Catholic Church* and finally entreat him to give its faithful and zealous clergy a full measure of ecclesiastical rights and an emancipation from the absolute government of missionary discipline in every diocese in which the settled conditions and numerical strength of congregations justify it. If a true representation of the condition of the American clergy be told before the coming council with some voice to state their wrongs and advocate their rights, there can be no doubt but that success will crown the issue.

By the first week in March 1869, *The Freeman's Journal* began to receive what the editor described as "triple the normal number of letters to the editor" on the topics aired by Jus. O'Callaghan answered the negative thrust in these letters which he synthesized in this manner: "Laymen and editors should mind their own business. The bishops can attend to these matters. They do not need the advice of laymen." His view of personal responsibilities in the Church he brought into clearer focus in this letter of March 20, 1869:

. . . Now none can believe more firmly than I that bishops have been commissioned by God to govern the Church. But does it follow from this that a bishop can do no wrong, or that he always governs wisely? I believe also that God committed to each of us the obligation of saving his own soul. This duty should demand as much care and attention from us individually as the duty of governing the Church should demand from any bishop. But does it follow that we are divinely commissioned to save our souls that we all do so? May it not also happen that a bishop notwithstanding his divine appointment, may neglect or ignore his duty?

As long as the individual bishops may err and actually do err, may it not happen that the government of some may be negatively if not positively injurious to religion, and if so, pray whose duty is it, if not the priests' to react. It cannot be denied that Rome desires that the American bishops would introduce parishes believing that the welfare of the American Church would be thereby promoted. Now if a priest should re-echo the voice of Rome, is he to be muzzled because some good souls are 'perfectly willing to leave all to the bishops?'

I will admit that bishops, not priests have been appointed to govern the Church. I will further assert that bishops, not priests have been appointed as judges of faith. But suppose a bishop or even more, a provincial bishop erred not only in matters of government, but also in matters of faith, would an objector possess his soul in peace and say,

'I am perfectly willing to leave all to the bishop, and obsequiously follow him to the devil?' I think not.

Now questions of faith are more important than questions of discipline, and a bishop has much less right to interfere in them, and still there may be times when the happy priest would be obliged to speak out and even act against his bishop. Otherwise he would act against his God. Hence, the position of those who object to this discussion is not only falacious but vicious.

IX

A month later, on April 24, 1869, O'Callaghan took a new tack in the Jus theme. He began with the American idea of freedom under law. And then he made a plea for due process in the light of American law, for American priests involved in canonical disciplinary cases with their bishops. Here was an idea totally new in its articulation on the American scene. Then he urged American priests to unite and make some form of petition to Rome during the upcoming Council to change their status. And lastly, in this letter, he took a more serious view of the few negative letters *The Freeman's Journal* was getting in response to Jus. These letters saw Jus as a troublemaker, but he replied that scandals do not come out of thin air but rather, are caused by the present system and will get worse if the system is not changed to conform with true Church law.

No other society in existence, political or religious, guards with such jealousy the rights of its humblest subject as does the Catholic Church, where its venerable laws have full influence. In no other country in the world is there more need of manifesting the liberty and protection which these laws yield, than in the United States, and yet *mirabile dictu,* perhaps in no country in the world is there exhibited such absolute and irresponsible autocracy on the part of bishops. If we only had the discipline which the Council of Trent enacted and established, then could priests boast with pride of the panoply of protection with which the Catholic Church clothes her humblest child.

Indeed, one would think the late Plenary Council of

Baltimore would do something towards guaranteeing to priests a trial in case of accusation. But no such thing! In fact it only seems to mock the helplessness of the priest by telling him that after being hanged (suspended), the bishop who played the triple role of judge, jury, and hangman may, if he choose, then grant him a trial! Exactly; here then is the law at present. Hang a priest first; then, if you wish, try him afterwards. (Vid. Con. Plen. Balt., Art. 77, p. 57.) Hear it, priests of America! Your whole hope, and claim, and title to an impartial trial, no matter how innocent you may be, absolutely depends on the mere condescension of the bishop, and this only after you are hanged (suspended), *'Si Episcopo videatur.'*

But let us suppose that a bishop, after hanging a poor priest, graciously condescends to give him a trial, and a jury of three are selected for that purpose; what will be the result? Will this jury, or any of its members declare in favor of the already degraded priest, even though innocent, and thereby pronounce the bishop a spiritual murderer who hanged an innocent priest? If a juryman did this, would he not thus effectually put his own neck in the halter? What prevents this bishop from hanging any one of this jury that differs from him in judgment? May he not justify himself on the plea that this juryman was conspiring against the authority of the bishops; and if one of this jury were hanged for his difference of judgment, do you think another jury would have one amongst them who would differ from his bishop? Henry VIII once tried this threat, even with his haughty Parliament, and it succeeded admirably; all thenceforth agreed with him. In the same way may a bishop, who acts unjustly towards a priest, compel a jury to ratify his sentence and approve his acts. How different would the case be if the bishop were ordinarily powerless until every accused priest was first pronounced guilty, not by the bishop but by the priests duly appointed to try him?

Our recollection, alas! admonishes us of the frequency of scandals for many years past; and the experience of every man of judgment, whether founded on his own observation or on the teachings of history, must convince him that these scandals must increase in frequency and magnitude, so long as the present unwise system of discipline is persevered in. 'Great oaks from little acorns grow.' The gale from the continuance and increase of the originating cause becomes the hurricane that sweeps destruction in its course, and leaves behind it only ruin and desolation. It behooves, therefore, bishop, priest and layman, every lover of order and religion, to bestir himself in applying the only specific for the prevention of this evil, (of arbitrary rule) which specific is no other than the full canonical establishment of parishes amongst us.

It speaks, therefore, a superabundance of petty malice for those who object to these articles to shift the odium of the Chicago and Auburn scandals [4] upon *The Freeman's Journal* and the advocates of parishes. If this nefarious and untruthful charge be repeated it will be the bounden duty of all concerned in the imputation, to enumerate the long, long list of such scandals that have lately occurred, and rehearse the causes that originated them, and which it were better let sleep in oblivion. If the objector will thus maliciously stigmatize those priests that advocate the establishment of parishes in America, it will be justifiable for the

---

4. In Auburn, New York and in Chicago pastors had refused to leave their rectories when reassigned by their respective bishops. A letter to the Editor of the Freeman's Journal which McMaster published, said that these incidents — which, in the Spring of 1869 were scandalous — were the direct result of the first Jus Letter.

hundreds of priests through the Union to rake up all the scandals of this sort that occurred in their respective dioceses during the last twenty years, and the causes that occasioned them, and perhaps those who object to Jus may learn that other causes than *The Freeman* were at the bottom of those evils. It is better then, to discuss this subject on its merits, or be silent . . . .

During the last week of April and the first week of May 1869, *The Freeman's Journal* began to receive a heavier volume of protest letters, mostly from clergy, regarding the Jus Letters. The most critical was published in the May 1st issue and was signed "Two or Three Sincere Friends."

McMaster wrote O'Callaghan that he thought the authors of this letter were bishops. The burden of the letter was that problems, scandals and inequities existing in the basic relationship between bishops and priests were matters far too delicate to be ventilated in the public press. Moreover the author of this letter said that bishops and priests throughout the country were offended by the comparison Jus had made between "hanging" and "suspension."

O'Callaghan replied on May 15, 1869. He did not in any way withdraw his basic thesis, but carried it further and explained it in greater detail. But he also explained why he was doing this — to let the bishops know what at least a substantial number of American priests were thinking, because, he said, he believed that if bishops really knew how the priests felt, they (the bishops) would be the first to lead the Church in America towards a greater freedom under law.

I am sorry that I have offended your 'two or three sincere friends.' Indeed, I do not wish to offend any one, but it seems to me 'sincere friends' ought not to be so thin-skinned. It would be impossible to write so as to please all. It must be remembered that when a man is full of a subject, he cannot be expected to sugar-coat every word he utters or writes. Christ himself, the exemplar of mildness, often used plain, unvarnished language in conveying unpleasant truths. This has an advantage; it strikes the understanding, and its impression upon the memory remains; while an idea stifled in the words that clothe it, is soon forgotten. Now, in my opinion, if *any cause demands forcible language it is the cause of the secular priests of America — the cause of law, instead of arbitrary will, of order instead of a state of submission, always liable to oppression and to consequent rebellion.*

It cannot be said that arguing against this anomalous state is apt to nurture disobedience. If it is wrong to argue against any existing human law or custom, it would be almost impossible to effect the least change in any condition of things, no matter how imperfect and mischievous such a condition may be; *for it is only in argument and discussion that the imperfections of any system are exposed,* and the advantages of a better state demonstrated and advocated. To deny this right of discussion in matters confessedly defective is *sheer tyranny,* of which no prelate in the Catholic Church would be guilty.

I would not insult our bishops by supposing them offended by the discussion of the present status of the clergy. I am convinced in my heart, if our bishops saw clearly that the interest of the Church required the introduction of law, they would themselves be foremost in the movement. I am also convinced if our bishops knew that a large majority of American priests desired the change, they would take the matter into immediate consideration. Believing this most conscientiously, I do not hesitate to use the strongest argument I can urge, couched in the strongest language I can command, to show the evils of the present exceptional system, and the advantages of the Catholic system of discipline. In doing so, I repose confidence in our prelates; I give them credit for sincerity and devotion to the interest of religion. In proof of my own sincerity, and my humble endeavors to labor for the cause of God, I may confidently appeal to those who know me.

Whilst, then, *I impute no sinister motives to the American Episcopate, I desire to be regarded as equally sincere in my convictions.* There is therefore, no covert attack made on any party, individually or collectively, but simply an inquiry into a state of government undoubtedly open and free to be criticized. I write against neither faith nor morals, but against a system manifestly imperfect, and permitted only by toleration of the Holy Father — against a system which he is most anxious to have superseded by Canon Law; against a system which the Council of Trent emphatically disapproves, and for the further continuance of which in America, the arguments for, are far less than the arguments against. I wonder, therefore, why your 'two or three sincere friends' have been annoyed, for I have not reasonably offended any one.

It seems to me, therefore, your 'two or three sincere friends' have been unnecessarily sensitive. Ever since Job's 'two or three sincere friends,' *we have daily example of well-meaning friends injuring the cause of God by their timidity and conservatism.* Let me assure them the word 'hang' was not introduced as a play on 'suspend,' but to establish a parallel — a thing to which no critic can object. Suspension means, literally, 'hanging'; but the similarity extends a great deal further. As hanging is one of the greatest punishments in the State, so is suspension one of the greatest punishments in the Church; as hanging deprives us of the use of our physical faculties, so does suspension deprive us of the legitimate use of our ecclesiastical and spiritual 'faculties'; as hanging brands with infamy the memory of its victims and disgraces his family, so does suspension brand a priest during life, even though afterwards rehabilitated, and imprints an indelible stigma on his family, which stigma the pious Catholic layman abhors more than death. I need not pursue the parallel further. *Now, as the civil law never 'hangs' a man, no matter how palpably guilty, without a fair, open, and impartial trial, so likewise our American Ecclesiastical law should not suspend a priest without a fair trial, unless in extraordinary cases.* To offer a trial after a priest is 'suspended,' is worse than mockery. I do not think, therefore, I was wrong in using the word 'hang' for 'suspend.' The words mean exactly the same, and the effects are exactly the same, each in its own order. Now, if I am justified in using 'hang' for 'suspend,' I am also right in using the cognate and correlative term of 'hang' whenever the sense requires it. To deny this right is to sweep away whole passages from the Bible, in which the same thing is repeatedly done.

Far from agreeing with your friends, I think this argument alone based on 'suspension' before conviction, should be sufficient to urge prelates to abolish this repulsive system. *The entire moral Code, as well as the Canons of the Church, presupposes that every man is innocent until proved guilty,* but by this *modus operandi* he is first not only supposed guilty, but even punished for the supposed guilt, and then perhaps he may by condescension get a chance to prove his innocence. Is such a system calculated to do good?

Perhaps after all I ought to thank your 'two or three friends' for affording me this opportunity of developing my meaning and explaining myself, for the present is a time we should rather conciliate than offend. Let me therefore ask the *priests of America,* are they content with the present system? It seems to me I hear a unanimous 'no' respond throughout the length and breadth of the Republic. Here, then, is the dilemma: Either we must be content or we must argue against the present system and expose its short-comings. Do your friends think that anyone would sincerely attack any system and deal it only feigned blows? My arguments may have little weight, but be that as it may, whenever I strike my heaviest blow I aim at the most vulnerable point as surest to gain my end. To do otherwise in a serious cause would be more herlequinade. . . . The *sooner priests speak their minds openly in the presence of their bishops the better.*

As I would not wish to live under a political government under which every man may be hanged without a trial, so likewise I do not like to live under an ecclesiastical government under which every priest may be suspended without a trial.[5] For my part, I am not content, nor will I be, until after the coming Council. If then America shall be regarded as unfit for a different discipline, I will, with all my soul, say 'Fiat.' However, in the meantime, the priests of America should bestir themselves to bring the question at an early day before the coming Council.

---

5. When this letter was written, O'Callaghan was working happily as pastor in Youngstown. But within the next two years, he was suspended twice without trial. In the first instance, he went to Rome where his appeal resulted in his vindication. In the second instance, he was unable to prepare for the trial that he asked for because of the *informata conscientia* clause in the suspension.

X

O'Callaghan did not write another Jus Letter for two months. Then, on July 17, 1869, he made an effort to analyze the reasons why he thought that the American bishops were arbitrary in their use of power. He also made an effort to tone down some of the reaction that the Jus Letters had caused among the younger clergy, especially priests from dioceses along the East coast who were writing to *The Freeman's Journal* that American bishops were "tyrants" and "despots." Worse, some were saying that these were characteristics of the Institutional Church itself.

O'Callaghan did not want to lose the interest and concern of these men, but he certainly did not want to have any part in some sort of clerical revolution or disaffection from the Church. He had this in mind when he wrote this seventh Jus Letter:

> . . . The Catholic Church forbids nothing but sin, or the proximate occasion of sin. Around 'life, liberty and the pursuit of happiness' she throws the aegis of her divine authority, and guards them against usurpation and oppression. Literature and the classics she has saved from the debris of ancient civilization, whilst the Arts and Sciences have ever found in her a steadfast guardian and benefactor. While these truths are incontrovertible, how comes it that Protestants regard the Church as inimical to liberty and intelligence?
>
> . . . While therefore the grand, self-sacrificing efforts made by Catholics in favor of education, completely refute

the calumny about Catholic love of ignorance, it cannot be denied that the abnormal relation of our bishops to our priests and laity seems to justify the Protestant opinion that the Church is the enemy of liberty.

But were I to grant — which I am not willing to admit — that our American bishops are despotic, it would by no means follow that the Catholic Church is despotic. Our difficulty is, that we are in a state of rapid transition, and we have almost grown to maturity while we are yet subject to a discipline suited to the infant state of the Church. Our condition is similar to that of a boy overgrown beyond his years, whose trousers that once extended below his ankles, now scarcely reach his knees, and whose jacket sleeves only reach his elbows, but who is yet made to move about in this ridiculous plight, and denied a suitable dress until nature, asserting her inexorable laws, bursts the bonds that confined him.

Our bishops are not free from the misfortune of all men in authority, which is to be surrounded by men who merely reflect the ideas and notions of the bishops themselves, and who have not independence enough to tell all the truth lest they should offend their masters or fall into disgrace themselves. Hence our bishops have unfortunately not always the means of learning the real condition of things, for it often happens that even those most aggrieved remain silent lest something worse may happen to them. It is, therefore, refreshing to find even one Journal independent enough to speak the truth even though unpleasant, and prudent enough to raise a warning voice against present evils which, if unattended to, must necessarily result in awful scandal.

I do not assert that our Prelates are despotic; I merely say that their very position and the dependent condition of those who ought to advise them, keep them in a fog. Those worthy counsel-men justify their criminal silence by the reflex principle that the bishop will have his own way anyhow, and hence it is useless for them to advise him; and besides, the Church, they say, is infallible, and all these mistakes will come right in the end. But they forget that the American Church is not infallible, and may go to the devil through their neglect. If there had been a regularly constituted chapter, and if priests were possessed of the independence (I use the term advisedly), which the laws of the Church grants them, they could speak plainly, and tell the bishop his duty and his danger, without fear of punishment. As long as this is not the case, bishops must blunder and their unfortunate position deserves our sympathy.

However, there remains the ugly fact of bishops' arbitrariness, which is a stumbling block to Protestants on their way towards the Church. Preach to them about the Church being the guardian of liberty, and they will laugh at you as long as they see a mitred Prelate play the absolute lord, spurn the prayers of his people and disregard their virtuous and pious wishes to be permitted to enjoy the direction of a priest who has won their love and confidence, and against whom there may be not a shadow of a charge. They will reply with a smile of pity; you eulogize the liberty of the Catholic Church while here in America the galling chains are chafing your very bones. We do not inquire how much liberty the Church grants her children in other countries, but we do know that their spiritual rulers do not allow them a very great measure here; therefore, 'before you ask us to become Catholics, physician cure thyself.' Such is the Protestant sentiment put into words, and every one must acknowledge that it has its prejudicial influence. But admitting the truth of all that is said, what follows? Simply that our American bishops are arbitrary and rule without law — nothing more. The spirit of the American laity, as well as the clergy of the Second Order, is opposed to this lawless rule; the Council of Trent is strongly opposed to it, Rome has given repeated proof, even within the last few years, that she is opposed to it. What force, therefore, has the objection?

Another evil feature of this abnormal system is that it not only prevents Protestants from coming into the Church but it drives Catholics out of the Church. This arbitrary rule gradually weakens the faith of shallow minded and un-instructed Catholics, while our enemies are ever on the alert in representing the Church to them as the enemy of liberty and pointing to these high-handed acts of arbitrary will, justify their charges. By thus appealing to the sacred names of Law and Liberty, as opposed to arbitrary will and slavery, they soon inveigle these poor, foolish Catholics, out of the Church, or what is tantamount to the same, they make them semi-infidel in the Church.

But this is not yet all. The exercise of this irresponsible and arbitrary power foments dissatisfaction and discord in the Church, for it offends the very best and most practical Catholics. It therefore aims a blow against the very unity of the Church, for which unity our Divine Lord so earnestly prayed. Hence the present system has, in addition to all that has been hitherto said against it, this threefold evil:

1. It tends to prevent the conversion of non-Catholics.

2. It tends to promote the perversion of Catholics.

3. It offends the very best of Catholics.

There is scarcely a priest or layman that cannot testify

to the truth of these conclusions, and even point out instances to illustrate them. I cannot therefore understand why our venerable Prelates petitioned Rome for the continuance of the present system 'for twenty years, or even forever' *'viginti annos vel in perpetuum'* — (vide Plen. Conc. Balt. secund. cxxxix 14.) But Rome refused to grant this strange petition as may be seen from the same passage. God bless Rome.

XI

On July 31, 1869, Father O'Callaghan published his eighth Jus Letter. It was centered on the mandate of the Council of Trent that wherever the Church finds herself in a stable condition, local bishops are "commanded to establish permanent parishes and place over them parish priests who are immovable." Our present Code of Canon Law has rendered this specific issue irrelevant today.

But on August 28, 1869, O'Callaghan published a ninth Jus Letter which was a rather profound discussion of the relationship which should exist between priest and bishop in the order of virtues that should mark both. He began with a quote from Isaiah, Ch. 5:1-7. Then he described the advantages that a bishop has in effecting community in a newly-established American Diocese. The unique thrust of this letter was to be found in its emphasis on what we call today subsidiarity and collegial responsibility.

If God should raise some favored mortal to an earthly throne, in order to give him a foretaste of the happiness and glory of the elect reigning with Christ, and, the better to complete this happiness, should permit him to choose his own subjects — those that would conduce most to the glory and happiness of his reign — whom may we suppose would he, if a wise man, select?

It seems to me this ideal kingdom would be composed of subjects distinguished especially for wisdom, intelligence, and piety, as the qualities most necessary in subjects to reflect upon their sovereign honor, happiness, and glory.

The subjects of a Bishop —those he has to govern — are his priests, and these only; for if he governs his priests well and wisely, the laity will follow not only with docility, but with joy. None will deny the truth of this statement; therefore, I will consider a bishop in his diocese as having priests only for subjects, and in this sense will I regard his government. Who can be supposed to possess piety, intelligence, and wisdom in a higher degree than the priests of God, the subjects of this spiritual Ruler? Even of these priests this Ruler has had the selection and the choice, either by himself or by his predecessor. Furthermore, he recruits their ranks from the most virtuous youths of his diocese, those distinguished for qualities most desirable to make his reign happy, and at a tender age he places them first in a college or preparatory seminary, next in his theological seminary, in which, apart from the world, beneath his own eye, and under the immediate and constant supervision of a director of his own choice, the young Levites are trained for many long years in all those duties and virtues desirable to make their Ruler happy — are, in fact, trained after his own ideal. Moreover, the limited number of these subjects, and their being under his own immediate and direct government, is another advantage in the hands of a wise governor; and, furthermore, the fact that these subjects have personal and selfish reasons for rendering prompt obedience, gives an additional advantage to this spiritual Ruler. Instead then, of exciting the suspicion and anxiety of their subjects; instead of occasioning confusion and scandal, by the exercise of arbitrary rule, why do they not, with all these extraordinary advantages, make their subjects happy, by governing according to law, and, by doing so, secure their own happiness by the reciprocal affection which this would evoke? Could any ruler ask for more favorable auspices? Could even imagination picture more desirable conditions?

None will deny that Bishops have the selection of their subjects; none will deny that they have the early training of their future subjects; none will deny that their subjects are distinguished for piety, intelligence, and wisdom. *They are the peers of their bishop in these qualities;* and in saying this I honor the episcopate, for I readily grant that bishops are selected from the clergy for the excellence of these gifts. *The priests of today are the bishops of tomorrow;* but let me remind these priests of today, while yet the equals of their unfortunate fellow subjects, that when they become bishops tomorrow they leave behind them, perhaps in the obscurity of humility, priests who are by no means their inferiors in knowledge, piety, and wisdom.

Does it not, then, appear most evident that bishops could, if they would, make not only their priests but themselves truly happy? *And yet why is it that so many bishops wear a crown of thorns beneath their mitres?* My deliberate conviction is that the cause lies chiefly in the system unhappily pursued by the bishops themselves. Not all the gifts, graces, and favors, natural and supernatural, given to Solomon, made him happy, because he not only strayed from the law of God but even from the law of reason; and not all the privileges, advantages and prerogatives possessed by American bishops can make their government happy, because they persist in a system of government which, under present circumstances, does not only not accord with the spirit of the Church, but is even opposed to reason.

I do not desire to offend even the hypercritical in saying that bishops pursue a course of government contrary to reason. I do not desire to attach any odium to bishops, collectively or individually, nor do I presume to set up my own judgment as the tribunal before which men every way my superiors must be judged. I simply appeal to the general dissatisfaction of both clergy and laity, and conclude that it is unreasonable to persist long in a system of government that has gotten such general dissatisfaction among the clergy of the Second Order, who are the peers of those of the First Order in all those qualities and requirements that contribute to make either a good subject or a good Ruler. The clergy could point out numerous wrongs and scandals proceeding from this system, which for charity's sake must be left unmentioned. Now and then, however, some scandal becomes known, to the great disturbance of the equanimity of our bishops and the great scandal of the laity. Bishops may not be aware of this general discontent, but nevertheless it exists, and their misfortune is that they place themselves in a position in which they cannot learn how odious they make themselves until it may be too late to apply a remedy. They may ignore this reasonable dissatisfaction, or, like Pharaoh, they may, on becoming acquainted with it, aggravate it in order to show their power; but this may not be wise statesmanship, nor wise episcopacy. If this course be persevered in, the *time may come when opposition to the arbitrary rule of bishops may insensibly pass into opposition to the order of bishops itself*. The grade from legitimate complaint when unheeded, into heresy, is easy, has often ere now been traveled; the devil never fails to take advantage of every loophole through which to drag souls into hell.

Arbitrary rule may be tolerated and even justified where subjects are simple and ignorant; indeed it may be perhaps demonstrated, that in the hands of good and wise men it may be the best rule for such subjects. But I not only affirm but maintain that arbitrary rule will never succeed with subjects distinguished for intelligence, wisdom, and

piety, as are the subjects of bishops. The Infinite alone can
rule arbitrarily and rule wisely. God only can follow His
own counsel in His dealings with His subjects and yet retain their love and obedience. A bishop ought not to rely
so much upon his own wisdom to disregard the advice of
his counsellors in matters concerning the spiritual welfare
of both priests and laity. He has, indeed, counsellors *in
nomine tantum,* but not if he treat them as the pagans sometimes treated their gods — rebuke them if their decisions
differ from his own, and spurn their deliberations to follow
his own darling ideas — is it then to be wondered that the
counsellors of a bishop say: O, these councils are all a
humbug and a farce; *we and the bishop understand each
other, the bishop never thinks of accepting our deliberate
advice, hence we never think of deliberating;* we are called
in simply to say — yes, to whatever the bishop proposes
and by doing this we save a double annoyance. I have heard
priests from various dioceses, counsellors of their respective
bishops, speak thus in substance, and I believe there is not
one of my clerical readers of three years' standing, that
cannot attest the same. While this may be true in general,
I am happy to state on information, that there are marked
and distinguished exceptions, and among some of the most
eminent of our Prelates. *Whilst these cases cheer us in the
desert, would it not be more preferable that in Church
government there should be no desert!*

In fact, arbitrary rule must necessarily be abused in the
hands of any man, not protected against this danger by
divine direction. Individual bishops do not claim this divine
aid in matters of faith, much less in matters of discipline.
God alone can wield so irresponsible a power. And even
God does not rule arbitrarily on earth. He binds Himself
by firm obligations to his subjects — in a manner in which

no bishop in the land condescends to bind himself — and this God of infinite power, wisdom, and knowledge, is bound to fulfill His own part of the obligation as long as His subject, a mere worm of the earth, *fulfills his part of the compact.* In other words, *God, almighty and infinite, rules by law,* not by arbitrary will, our bishops, finite and fallible, rule by arbitrary will, not by law. *As subjects of an All-wise and Omniscient God, we have rights which He is bound to respect;* but as subjects of American bishops, and their equals in knowledge, wisdom and piety, 'we have no rights which they are bound to respect.' Is this an orderly condition of things in a country where there are rich and permanently established dioceses? It is hard to be calm when treating of such a subject.

In order to appreciate this system fully, let us consider the priest in the three-fold character of intelligence, wisdom, and piety, and ascertain, as well as we may, how arbitrary rule accords with any of them.

Priests have intelligence; knowledge is with them a *quality sine qua non.* 'The lips of the priest shall keep knowledge.' They need it in the exercise of their profession; they spend, even as does the bishop, their whole lifetime in its pursuit; and were they not possessed of it, the bishop would sin mortally in permitting them to minister to a congregation; he should immediately withdraw their faculties. They know what the law is as well as their bishop does; they know his duties as well as he knows theirs. Even in a missionary country, they know where legitimate authority ought to stop and where usurpation may begin; they know the weaknesses and prejudices of human nature, and are able generally to assign acts to their true motives, no matter what ostensible reasons may be given to justify them. And it is hard for intelligent subjects, thus instructed, to submit to acts justified by no law, and perpetrated simply in the absence of all law, and proceeding solely from the head of one not much more distinguished for knowledge than either of themselves. The ignorant and the simple may not always distinguish between law and arbitrary will, but it is otherwise with the intelligent; and with priests, who are the peers of their bishops in knowledge, *every act unwarranted by law, even if that law does not exist here, is noticed,* and a persistence in such acts must urge every intelligent subject to seek by legitimate means the discontinuance of such an odious system. Hence intelligence must condemn this system of arbitrary rule.

Next, which side does wisdom take in this question? Wisdom must be a distinctive quality of the secular priest, for without it he is unfit, no matter how great his intelligence, to govern his people. Now wisdom must condemn this arbitrary rule, for it is the *part of wisdom to follow the councils of the great and the venerable of the past,* strengthened as they were by the Holy Ghost, rather than the feeble light of our own judgment, especially when we find a very great number at the present time urging us to such a course. It is the part of wisdom to provide what is most expedient to reach its end, and to foresee the causes of disorder and eliminate them. It is the part of wisdom to regulate all things according to divine law, and canon law; wisdom will not advocate the propriety of giving to any fallible man, in the government of subjects, as pious, as wise, and as intelligent as himself, more arbitrary power than God himself exercises over his subjects. *This arbitrary rule has occasioned much evil, and will, every year that it continues, occasion greater evils;* for it will be growing more and more abnormal, and must be condemned by the voice of wisdom, which is the advocate of law and order. 'Counsel and equity is mine,' says wisdom, 'by me kings reign and lawgivers decree just things. By me princes rule and the mighty decree justice.' A man of common sense and ordinary judgment governing by law and guided and protected by law, may pass through life as a good ruler, and merit, while living, the love of his subjects and their affectionate, prayerful, remembrance after his death. But a man ruling by arbitrary power, no matter how great his wisdom, and disinterested his intentions, may do irreparable injury be-before he knows it.

Is there none of our bishops who has ever done an imprudent act in governing? Is there none of them who can look back through his episcopacy and say: had I to begin again I would not repeat all my former acts of arbitrary power? Of course bishops only can answer this; yet their subjects may guess at the answer. Whilst then a ruler of ordinary powers may make himself and his subjects happy, a ruler even with extraordinary capacity, no matter how good his intentions, and disinterested his motives, must make many great mistakes; for the exercise of this most extraordinary power requires the possession of extraordinary wisdom, which God vouchsafes to few men. His position is the realization of the fable of Phaëthon attempting to guide the chariots of the sun, and succeeding only in bringing ruin upon himself and a part of the world as the price of his temerity. *None but God can exercise arbitrary power wisely and beneficially.* Hence wisdom must condemn this system of arbitrary rule.

Now let us see, in favor of which side of this controversy will piety declare. *The Priest must be pious;* he is the salt of the earth and the light of the world, even as the bishop. Now piety abhors arbitrary rule, for it can be never opposed to both wisdom and intelligence. Piety would inaugurate a system that would save the ruler from blunders that do evil, and would save the subject from injurious interference; (a system) that would stimulate zeal, and lessen if not prevent the occasions of scandal — in a word, piety would introduce order and would illustrate the beauty of the Catholic Church by pointing to the wisdom of her laws. *Piety would establish law, order and harmony, in order to prepare a suitable field for itself wherein to flourish, and to show that Christ's kingdom on earth is the ante-chamber of His kingdom in heaven.* Hence piety must condemn this abnormal system of arbitrary rule.

If then the most honorable and the most enviable Ruler is he whose subjects are distinguished for piety, wisdom and intelligence, such a ruler, to be happy must govern by law, not by arbitrary will; and since the subjects of a bishop must possess these qualities in a pre-eminent degree, it follows that there is urgent necessity for changing our arbitrary rule into a system of law.

But some one may ask, why have you not included obedience in your list of qualifications of subjects? For the simple reason that *it is not a principal but an accessory quality. Obedience, if not directed by piety, intelligence and wisdom, is not a virtue but a vice;* and be assured that where subjects are possessed of piety, intelligence and wisdom, *obedience is sure to follow* unless it is the fault of the Ruler or the system he pursues.

This arbitrary rule brings evil not to the subjects only, it makes the bishop himself far more unfortunate and his condition far less enviable. He is left without a guide, without a safeguard, he is subject to become the victim of his own impulses, his prejudices and his rash conclusions; he will make changes and removals 'for the good of religion,' when both the priest and people respectfully protest, and when, if his secret motives were scrutinized, perhaps the urgent cause that moved him to such a course was some grudge, some supposed personal indignity to avenge, some pet arbitrary measure to carry out; and yet, while doing this, he really may be in good faith, think he is acting dispassionately and solely 'for the good of religion.' It is surprising how far passions blind us; when sifted down it is alarming to find how much selfishness there is mingled with our best and most disinterested actions. The position of such a Ruler is an awful one, not merely accountable for the bodies but the souls of thousands. He is a ship without a rudder, driven about by every wind of the varying notions of his own mind. He is brought in relation with subjects, equally as intelligent, as wise, as pious, and as devoted as himself. *He comes into collision with some of them.* If he strikes he may be wrong and do much evil, if he does not strike he may be wrong and do much evil.

... As matters are at present, I believe there is no position in which a priest could be placed in which he should be so miserable as on the episcopal throne.

XII

From August to November 1869, Jus remained silent. During this time, Father O'Callaghan was forced to face himself and re-evaluate what was his most prized possession, his integrity. The events which forced this re-evaluation created a situation where he found himself victim of many of the very things the Jus Letters had said could happen to an American priest under the Missionary system.

Bishop Rappe, in 1867, had issued a circular letter in which he decreed that any parish which did not pay in full its assessment for the support of the Diocesan seminary would be denied the services of a priest. This is precisely what happened to St. Columba's in Youngstown, O'Callaghan's parish, in September 1869. The collection was thirty-five dollars short of the one hundred eighty dollar tax, so the bishop punished the parish and transferred O'Callaghan to Lima, Ohio.[6]

O'Callaghan asked the Archbishop of Cincinnati for advice. Archbishop Purcell, who had no real jurisdiction over such a

---

6. Bishop Rappe's Law regarding the Seminary Tax had been assailed at Rome by large numbers of the clergy of Cleveland as early as 1868 and was abrogated by the Propaganda in April-May, 1870. The primary reason for clergy opposition to the law was the sanctions which it contained. These were:

1) Any pastor who failed to accurately report the number of families in his congregation by as few as four was *ipso facto* suspended.

2) Any parish which failed to meet the tax imposed upon it according to the number of families reported was deprived of the services of a priest.

Propaganda Archives, Cong. America Centrale, Vol. 23, pp. 347, 348.

local matter, urged Bishop Rappe to "take care, lest the episcopacy become odious to Catholic Americans." [7]

But Bishop Rappe did not back down. Bolstered by his law,
he carried out O'Callaghan's transfer. But O'Callaghan said this
was an act of arbitrary use of power and he asked to appeal to
Rome against what he called "degradation without cause."

On November 20, 1869, the tenth Jus Letter was published
in *The Freeman's Journal*. In this letter, O'Callaghan makes a
brief reference to the very situation in which he then found himself. In discussing the need for tenure and permanency as psy-
chological supports (he called them "spiritual"), for a priest
in the fruitful exercise of his office. He wrote:

> Let us examine the conditions in the American Church
> especially. A priest, no matter how faithful in the discharge
> of his duty, how beloved by his people, or how esteemed
> by his non-Catholic fellow-citizens, is liable at any moment
> to be moved by the caprice or personal pique of the bishop.
> There is no alternative for the priest; no law, no court, no
> trial, no jury of peers, no fixed rights. He is ordered presto
> from perhaps the best to the worst mission in the Diocese.
> If he refuses, he is suspended and disgraced before the
> people. If he obeys and goes, he is also disgraced in the
> estimation of the people who will think that such a removal
> could not be ordered without grave reasons, and who are
> free, in fact, to imagine whatever crime they please as a
> presumptive cause.

O'Callaghan then made oblique notice of how he personally felt in such a situation.

---

7. O'Callaghan to A. Cardinal Barnabo, *Propaganda Archives, Cong.
America Centrale,* Vol. 23, p. 336.

Thus the people are scandalized. But the priest is *profoundly discouraged,* and he suffers in his person and his reputation.

He had said often, his "reputation was dearer than life itself, to me." These words were enough on this painful subject. He went on as Jus to make an appeal to American Priests for action. But, perhaps to avoid the danger of campaigning for his own personal cause, he stressed that the decision was theirs. He began:

> The present system of discipline is not only negatively, but even positively injurious to religion in many of the United States . . .

> To act or not to act, this is the question. Let the priests of America seriously consider it. Any manifestation of their desire, couched in humble and respectful language, breathing the spirit of charity, professing unalterable attachment to the Holy See and petitioning for protection and law, would I have no doubt, receive a favorable hearing at Rome, and move the heart of the saintly Pius IX.

This letter, written just as he was sailing for Rome from New York with a double identity in a sense, as the promoter of the Jus cause, now already more than a year old, and as a pastor trying to regain his parish in Youngstown, might well have been very difficult to write. Up to this point, the Jus themes had been, for O'Callaghan, quite theoretical; now the possibilities they envisioned were happening to him. The irony of the whole thing must have been that he could not share his anxiety with anyone except the three or four men who knew who Jus really was.

If he had complained of loneliness in his Youngstown

missions, this new loneliness must have been much more acute. Surely few men went to Rome at the opening of Vatican I with more cause for anxiety and less interior peace.

But as Jus, O'Callaghan did outline a plan in the form of a petition for the American clergy, who had responded so favorably to the Jus themes for the past year, for their endorsement. He seems to have had great confidence that this petition would be heard and granted by the Pope. It was worded in this way:

1) That every priest who has, for seven years, been engaged in the care of souls without reproach, shall be inamovable, except for due cause.

2) That no priest shall be punished, except by temporary suspension, unless on the sentence of the *Judices Causarum* of the diocese in due process.

3) That the *Judices Causarum* of the diocese be named one by one by the Ordinary of the diocese each year, according to the provisions of the Council of Trent. Since our bishops have no Chapters of dioceses; that as the nearest thing to it, the priests who have attained the position of inamovability, except for cause, shall have the right in the Annual Synod, to approve or reject any of the *Judices Causarum,* named one by one by the Ordinary.[8]

---

8. This was a specific appeal for some new form of canonical legislation which would bridge the "Cathedral Chapters" envisioned by the Council of Trent and the developing maturity of the American Church while it still held Mission status. *C. F.* Council of Trent, *SESS XXIV de Refor.*

In a Jus Letter published July 31, 1869, O'Callaghan made reference to the mandate of the Council of Trent regarding appointment of permanent pastors who, after seven years, would become candidates for the office of *Judices Causarum* which he translated in this form: "In both those cities and places where parochial churches do not have definite boundaries nor do they have rectors who rule their own people,

Since over one thousand American priests had written to *The Freeman's Journal* in support of Jus, both the Editor, McMaster, and probably O'Callaghan, expected that these same one thousand priests would put their names to this petition. It asked no more — in fact much less — than many priests wanted. It was canonical; it should carry some weight in Rome.

Very few priests signed the petition, however. Perhaps McMaster never made it really clear how they were to do so. Perhaps, because they did not know who Jus was, they were not willing to take the chance of making their names public in Rome where their bishops, whom in a few cases they may have feared, were gathered. Perhaps the issue was too vague and limited in its goals, and there was no certainty it would even be heard by Roman authorities.

In any case, the course O'Callaghan followed in Rome to pursue the themes he had articulated in the Jus Letters remains obscure to this day. Certainly it would seem he faced serious obstacles. His course was especially difficult because he was appealing his own case at the same time. And surely the Curia and the Cardinal Prefect of the Propaganda were very preoccupied with the business of the Council.

Recognizing the need for some form of constituency, O'Callaghan wrote his eleventh Jus Letter probably while he was on board ship. It was published December 4, 1869. In this

---

but who administer the sacraments in a haphazard way to those seeking them, this holy Synod of Bishops for the greater care of the souls committed to them assigns to each one their own perpetual and particular pastor so that there be a distinct congregation and certain parishes of their own who must know them and from whom alone they may licitly receive the sacraments. And for a further reason, that he may provide for the exigencies according to the quality and needs of the place. At the same time, in those cities and places where there are no parishes, this holy Synod orders that they be begun immediately all customs and immovable privileges notwithstanding." *Idem Caput XII.*

letter, he summed up in language more polemical than he had previously used, the general theme of rights for American priests. He pointed out that the deprivation of these rights was indirectly, injurious to the bishops and the episcopacy in general. Then he made a strong plea for the petition which would, Jus said, demonstrate to the Roman Curia the solidarity of American priests behind the three proposals he had published in the letter of November 20. The style of this letter seems different from previous Jus Letters. But it failed to inform the priests who would read it that Jus was already on his way to Rome, nor did the letter say that a representative of Jus will go to Rome. It did say this:

Since we have every reason to suppose that Rome is not opposed to our ideas, it is of the highest importance that someone having the cause at heart be sent to Rome. He may not be a personage of great importance, yet his presence there may avail much. We know from Ecclesiastical History that in past times, God often used the voice of a child or even the movement of a brute beast to indicate His will and became the beginning of movements that even yet benefit the world. The contemptible things of this world does God use to confound the mighty. So let there be a voice at Rome, no matter how low it may whisper; let there be a representative of our ideas there, no matter how simple he may be. It is not an imposing presence and lofty conversation, but the goodness of his cause that recommend him. The importance of this question and the importance of the present time alike demand a representative. Who shall he be? When shall he go? How shall he be sent? I leave this to others to discuss these questions.

But if the priests of the United States will make no move in the present acceptable time they will forcibly remind me of those who lived in the time of Noe; they not only saw the ark building and mocked the folly of the builder, but even when it was almost afloat and they might have entered it, they refused, each preferring to paddle his own canoe and trust to the mercy of the vacillating waves.

For nearly a year, Jus had urged that someone from the American Clergy go to Rome during the Council. The reaction had been an almost unanimous response that Jus be the one to go. Now Jus was at Rome, but it would seem in his own behalf first. Still he never seems to have forgotten that he was Jus. And he continued to preserve his anonymity successfully.[9] If one looks closely at this letter, it appears clear, at least in retrospect, that his own problems and the cause of Jus are equally important to him since the former is a result of what the latter said would happen without law to protect American priests.

O'Callaghan recapitulated the arguments he had stated previously in the eleventh Jus letter adding just one new twist. He made allusion to the bishop, when he is the Ordinary of a diocese, as the Apostle of the diocese both in law and in fact. Then he said that most American bishops were cast in the role of Vicars Apostolic implying they had no permanent community to serve and that, as a result of this role, the bishops were deprived of the real grace that God gives to the fullness of Apostleship.

If the American bishops while they were at home had not been aware of the Jus Letters, or if they did not take the

---

9. Bishop Bernard McQuaid of Rochester, N.Y. writing from Rome to his Vicar General, Father James Earley on April 24, 1870, noted: "No one here has been able to discover the representative of Jus." C. F. *Documents of American Catholic History*, ed. by John Tracy Ellis, Bruce 1955, p. 404.

whole campaign for Priests' Rights seriously, they became
quite alert to the possibility of the petition being given by
someone to Roman authorities during the Council. Bishop Mc-
Quaid wrote of their watchfulness and of his view of the whole
matter in a letter to Dr. Michael Corrigan on February 6,
1870:

> We are still waiting for the appearance of McMaster's
> champion of Priests' Rights. No one can make out who he
> is; certainly he has not made himself known as such, or
> in that character to anyone in authority. My own suspicions
> based on good reason, lead me to believe that I know him
> and that he has been here, but not as McMaster described;
> that he has done no more than represent, when he found
> opportunity, the great agitation in the United States, but
> never putting himself forth as the representative of any
> body. His character was such that no one suspected him,
> nor did we, until quite lately, know that he had trouble
> with his bishop. As the trouble is settled, it is probable
> that he will return to his diocese and try to conceal his
> part in the agitation. There is a priest here, O'Callaghan,
> of the Diocese of Cleveland but his trouble does not go
> beyond his own affair.[10]

------

10. *The Life and Letters of Bishop McQuaid,* by Frederick Zwer-
lein, Rome, Desclee and Campagni, Vol. II, p. 37. On the surface
this suggests several implications.
1) It would seem that Bishop McQuaid is given to greater candor in
writing to the President of Seton Hall than he demonstrates in writing
to his Vicar General Father Earley to whom he wrote two months later
saying nobody in Rome "has been able to discover the representative
of Jus."
2) Bishop McQuaid seems to think that he has discovered McMaster's
representative but he does not seem to think it is O'Callaghan whom he
notices but disregards as merely an aggrieved priest.
3) It never seems to have occurred to McQuaid that Jus himself was

The twelfth and final Jus Letter, published in *The Freeman's Journal* on March 26, 1870, was accompanied by a rather lengthy personal letter from O'Callaghan to McMaster dated from Rome, February 26, 1870.

O'Callaghan, in the letter to McMaster, apologized for whatever inconvenience the Jus series had caused the Editor. At the same time, he expressed a strong hope that they both might live long enough to see the fulfillment of what the Jus Letters had pleaded for; and he hoped the series had not been an annoyance but rather a prod to the American bishops. But above all, he asked McMaster to urge the petition among the priests of America. Finally, O'Callaghan urged McMaster to keep his presence in Rome and his identity a secret. Obviously, he wanted at all costs to avoid becoming a public figure in Rome; this could certainly have forced him into unwanted and unproductive controversy with various members of the American hierarchy who were in Rome at that time. He prodded McMaster to get the petition out and get it signed by the friends of the Jus cause. Then he concluded with his personal observation about the events taking place at the Council and in Rome.

This final Jus Letter continued to preserve the anonymity of the author. As O'Callaghan said thirty years afterwards, "The element of mystery is always a potent factor in arousing attention; it not only excites curiosity, but stimulates con-

---

in Rome.
4) One wonders how McQuaid can feel so certain the representative of Jus has made no presentation to anyone in authority in Rome. As was seen in Chapter II, O'Callaghan, reflecting in 1896 on the course of Jus at Rome in 1870, said he was in touch with two Curial Prelates, one of whom was a daily confidant of Pius IX. O'Callaghan said he spoke to this Prelate frequently "about the abnormal conditions in the American Church."

templation and energizes reflection. The consideration of what we are and what we ought to be, if leavened with prudence and perseverance, will always work improvement."

This letter urged upon the priests of America that what they hoped for, namely the protection of true law, they could have if they asked for it. Jus went on to explain that Rome was now aware that the Missionary stage of the Church in America, at least in the larger Dioceses, had ended, and that the gradual introduction of Canon Law in these dioceses was precisely what Rome wanted. The problem as far as Rome was concerned, was whether this was what the American priests wanted.

Jus went on to say it was true that some priests in America may abuse their new-found freedom, but argued that this is always to be expected in any large body of men newly made free. Moreover, full Canon Law made provision for such failures in a manner far more equitable than the Missionary system which made the rule of the bishop so totally arbitrary. Canon Law as Jus saw it, would protect the bishop from this pitfall, place his acts within the context of fixed law, and keep him close to his priests.

A new view of the transfer of priests from one parish to another was reflected when Jus wrote:

If at any time a bishop sees that a certain priest of his diocese is, in the language of one of Jus' critics, 'the right man for the right place'; if he (the bishop), needs him for a trying or difficult mission, let the bishop ask such a priest to go. My word for it, notwithstanding inamovability, few good priests would refuse. Let it be understood that the post of danger and of labor is the post of honor, and our priests will go. The very places which today priests refuse unless compelled absolutely, would be joyfully accepted and even sought . . . for the good priest is always capable of being heroic if he is asked to be so by his bishop . . . What the slave does with half a will, the free man does with joy.

We priests in America are not slaves who need the lash to make us do our duty. Are we so ignorant as to be unable to live by law instead of arbitrary will? Are we so vicious as to be unfit to be entrusted with law? Are our bishops so wise, so dispassionate, so infallible as to never abuse the dangerous power they now possess? Is the bishop invariably right and the priest invariably wrong?

Here again, O'Callaghan is struggling, one might suspect, with his feelings regarding his own situation at the hands of his bishop. As he always did in times of personal stress, he stressed the integrity of the priest and the corresponding trust the bishop should demonstrate towards his priests. Jus continued:

Must the bishops of other countries govern by law, and must it be an insult to the American bishops if we American priests petition the Holy Father that our bishops also be requested to govern by law? . . . Much as I admire the American bishops, I do not regard them as superior to those of France, Germany, Spain or Ireland, nor is our clergy inferior to the clergy of these countries. If this were true, then God help the Church in America, it is already too late for the power of the American bishops to save it.

Here Jus had interjected an interesting point, novel in his day. He saw the American Church as a special entity with a special mission and character and he, by implication, cut it off in its government from affinity to its European origins. At the same time, he professed a great loyalty to the Pope. In this vein, summing up the whole theme of Jus in hope, he says:

To argue for a continuance of arbitrary power is to

stigmatize the whole American Church. This is an insult
to the laity as well as to the clergy and it pays no great
compliment to the bishops themselves . . . . For over two
years, we have used every argument we could think of
to convince even a disinterested party, that the day of use-
fulness of the present system has passed . . . . The time has
come when a new system should be inaugurated if the
priests of the United States desire it.

At this point, O'Callaghan takes a sudden and quite new
direction. To conceal the fact that he was Jus and was in
Rome, he employed a tactic of diversion which, as we have
seen, deceived at least Bishop McQuaid. Indeed, it was not until
February 1896, that O'Callaghan publicly announced that he
was Jus. By that time, most of the American bishops who were
in Rome at the First Vatican Council in 1870, had died not
knowing the identity of the anonymous author who had hit so
hard at what he called their "arbitrary rule" nearly thirty years
earlier. One might wonder what those bishops who were still
living and had been at the Council thought of Jus' last announcement.

This diversionary tactic with which O'Callaghan ended his
final Jus Letter is best understood in his own words:

Most favorable accounts have been sent from Rome by
the priest who has undertaken to represent us there.

This is the first time that American priests had been made
aware that they did in fact, have a representative in Rome. This
sudden announcement may be, perhaps, the only blunder
O'Callaghan made in the whole Jus affair. It may well have been
disenchanting to many of the priests who espoused the Jus
cause and who wrote to *The Freeman's Journal* urging that Jus
himself be their representative in Rome. The implication was

that the task was in the hands of an unknown stranger and this might have cooled the enthusiasm of many priests who had supported Jus. But O'Callaghan seems to have had no other choice so long as he wished to remain anonymous. His letter went on as if he were writing in America:

> I have no doubt that he has acted wisely and well. He states upon authority not to be spurned, that the whole question as to whether we will have law instead of arbitrary government now depends entirely upon ourselves. What could be more cheering? Think of it, American priests, and remember that if we do our simple duty, a duty that involves neither expense nor peril, the Catholic Church will not continue under arbitrary rule in America *'for twenty years,'* much less *'forever,'* but this rule will cease to exist before one more year is out . . . . Rome, ever accessible to justice, law and reason, is waiting to hear our complaints — or has already heard them *and is only waiting to grant our petition . . . .*

To have spoken with such certitude on so serious a matter and quoting the most galling passages of the Baltimore Council of 1866 specifically, would seem to indicate either that O'Callaghan was merely indulging his hopes and dreams or that he had been informed in Rome that the abrogation of the Missionary status for the American Church could be granted immediately. What was necessary was a petition from the American priests. But the signed petition never came. O'Callaghan begs for it as Jus continues:

> No representative at Rome, no matter what his influence or wisdom, can effect any good without petitions. This is the burden of our Representative's letters; without petitions, we can effect nothing, or at least, very little . . . . The Holy Father will grant what we ask if it is signed by the majority

of the secular clergy of the United States . . . . If this happens, nothing is more certain than that success will crown our efforts . . . .

Considerable evidence to suggest that in 1870, Pope Pius IX and the Propaganda wanted an abrogation of the Missionary status in Law for the American Church at least in the more settled and well-established dioceses. If this was true, however, it does not seem demonstrable that this desire on the part of Roman authority was influenced by the Jus Campaign in *The New York Freeman's Journal*. But what does seem demonstrable is that Jus was aware that Roman authority did desire this change and he articulated precisely the context in which, it would seem, that authority indicated that the transition should occur, namely the gradual development of Cathedral Chapters in each American diocese.[11]

Here several questions arise which, for the present, seem impossible to answer. Did some highly influential Curial official indicate to O'Callaghan that the Holy See wanted some signal from the American clergy that would precipitate this action? In his final letter Jus said:

All Rome wants is to know whether the Status of Law is really desired by the priests of America. If the present status gives general satisfaction, although abnormal, Rome may not insist on a change, but if the majority of priests in America show by petition that the present status ought to be substituted by a government of Law, there is nothing more certain than that success will crown our efforts.

Will the priests of America let this golden opportunity pass? No one will have the occasion to refuse because of this or that proposition in the Petition for the pro-

---

11. *C. F. An American Anomaly: Bishops without Canons*, by Robert Trisco, *Chicago Studies*, Vol. 9, No. 2, pp. 143ff.

positions stated will be merely *suggestive*, leaving the Holy Father to alter or modify them as to him it seems best. Let no time be lost in forwarding this Petition because those whose influence may be of the highest value to us may leave Rome before our Petition would reach thither. Let every Priest induce a brother Priest to forward his name immediately so that we may show by an *overwhelming* majority that the time for Law has arrived . . . .

How does O'Callaghan know that the desire of the priests of America will be heard by the Holy Father? Why does he urge that the Petition be sent so quickly? Who is it that has such "influence" who may leave Rome shortly? Would the Roman authority be willing to overrule the body of American bishops whose petition on a given subject, in this case, Missionary status for the United States, if their position was in opposition to the wishes of the majority of the American priests?

Jus felt strongly that the answer to this last question was in the affirmative. He wrote as he summed up his hopes, in the final Jus Letter:

Let the priests of America remember that the Most Reverend Bishops of the late Plenary Council of America told us, it would appear, by way of apology, for their arbitrary government that the times do not yet permit a government according to law. This would at least give us a hope that at some future time we or our successors may be blessed by a government in accordance with law. Our prelates may plead before Rome that we are content, that a government that gives general satisfaction may be continued, etc. Let us show that this arbitrary rule does not give general satisfaction. Let us show not only the liability of this power to be abused, but that actual abuse has made it necessary for us to desire the protection of Law, and that, seeing that our Prelates propose to rule absolutely *'for ever,'* we have been compelled to have recourse to our Holy Father for an amelioration of our condition . . . .

Here were the canonical reasons why Jus felt the Petition should be submitted. These reasons were pragmatic at the same time. He was saying simply that the system did not work and that there was an option for a better system.

But O'Callaghan was not a revolutionary. He saw clearly enough, that as a missionary, he was a builder who would not necessarily see the final results of what was being built. He thought of American priests of a later time when he articulated his final hope:

> . . . If we could only hope that in twenty or thirty years that our prelates would relinquish arbitrary power and deign to govern by law, we might better be content; we might better obey any commands cheerfully no matter how severe; but to have *'for ever'* ringing in our ears tells us most eloquently that if we want law, we must *ask* for it.

Perhaps the most devastating question one might ask after reading all of this would be: has anything changed in the last one hundred years?

Significantly, it would seem Eugene O'Callaghan felt that the relationship between the First and the Second Order of the hierarchy in America had improved greatly between the time he wrote the Jus Letters in 1868-1870 and the time he revealed himself as Jus in 1896. There had come from Rome many norms for guiding these relationships, and the Third Plenary Council of Baltimore in 1884 granted many rights to American priests which it would be fruitless to enumerate here.

One final question remains. When O'Callaghan revealed himself as Jus to *The Freeman's Journal* in 1896, the Editor,

Father Louis Lambert, signed an editorial asserting that these articles of Jus lacking the petition of the American priests, which never came, did help bring about the establishment of an Apostolic Delegation in the United States in 1892. Father Lambert saw the Delegation as a compromise between the Missionary system of Law (which continued in this Country until 1908), and the full introduction of Canon Law that Jus petitioned for in 1870. The Apostolic Delegate came to America to mediate priest-bishop conflicts already existing. This he did rather successfully in the early years of the Delegation. Moreover, his task was to see that the bishops respected the rights of the priests of America in Law. This the Delegate did until the promulgation of the Code of Canon Law in 1917. One wonders if Rome waited for the petition of the American priests of which Jus spoke for twenty-two years and then, in exasperation sent a Delegate?

In any event, one would suspect that Father O'Callaghan would have rejoiced to see our time. The topics to which he gave the energy and clarity of his mind have broadened surely; rights, duties, due process and the continuing concern of the American Church regarding its missionary role in secular society are today matters which go a good deal beyond the bishop-priest relationship O'Callaghan addressed. But the participation of each individual in the Mission of the Church would draw his attention today. And he would urge, plead, chide, insist, appeal, remain faithful and never give up. For sure, the man who echoed the words, "How long, O Lord, how long?" would not be complacent or silent.

POSTSCRIPT

The Author realizes that many questions raised by this presentation remain unanswered and that several issues are presented ambiguously. To pursue these questions further would distract from the primary purpose of this book, however, which has been to reveal the life of Eugene O'Callaghan insofar as it can be discovered; to demonstrate that the unique character of his thought did not cause him to fail in any way to fulfill his essential vocation to the priesthood in the Missionary Diocese of Cleveland; and to ask the reader to think about the ideal of law which he envisioned which would, he thought, make American priests free.

Seldom has reference been made to source material in this text. But for those who may desire to know, copies of all the material herein quoted or consulted are in the possession of the Author. This material was located in the following places: University of Notre Dame Archives; Archives of the Archdiocese of Baltimore; Archives of the Diocese of Cleveland; Archives of the Sacred Congregation of the Propaganda, Rome; Newspaper files of the Public Libraries of Cleveland; New York; Youngstown, Ohio; Fremont, Ohio; and over one hundred interviews with people who remembered Eugene O'Callaghan personally.

While this work is historical in character, it is popular rather than technical in its format. It is not a biography of Father O'Callaghan, nor is it an attempt to present fully the Church he knew as it developed in the context of late nineteenth century.